Writing, Audio, & Video Activities

1

Writing Activities by	**Audio Activities by**	**Video Activities by**
Janice G. Darias	**Peggy Boyles**	**Mary de López**
Newton South High School	Foreign Language Coordinator	University of Texas at El Paso
Newton Centre, MS	Putnam City Schools	El Paso, TX
	Oklahoma City, OK	

ScottForesman

A Division of HarperCollins*Publishers*

Editorial Offices: Glenview, Illinois

Regional Offices: Sunnyvale, California • Atlanta, Georgia
Glenview, Illinois • Oakland, New Jersey • Dallas, Texas

Table of Contents

ISBN: 0-673-21675-6

Copyright © 1996

Scott, Foresman and Company, Glenview, Illinois

All Rights Reserved. Printed in the United States of America.

For information regarding permission, write to:

Scott, Foresman and Company, 1900 East Lake Avenue, Glenview, Illinois 60025.

12345678910-PT-I04030201009998979695

Front and Back Cover Photos: © Suzanne Murphy FPG International

Writing Activities

EL PRIMER PASO Fecha _____

A Ask four of your classmates what their names are, and then write down exactly what each one says. Follow the model.

Me llamo Susana.

1. _Tyker Williams_
2. _Bert Lynch_
3. _Michael Jones_
4. _Jacob Gregg_

Now, write down your own name:

Jennet Bun

B Look at the map and then write down the answer that each person would give to the question: *¿De dónde eres?* Follow the model.

Esteban: *Soy de Nicaragua.*

1. Alicia: _Soy de Guatemala_ .
2. Verónica: _Soy de Panama_ .
3. Arturo: _Soy de Costa Rico_ .
4. Benjamín: _Soy de Honduras_ .

1

EL PRIMER PASO Fecha

C Write the Spanish word for at least five objects in your classroom. If possible, try to name more. Don't forget to include *el, la, los,* or *las* with each word!

1. la television
2. la mesa
3. La ventana
4. La pizarra
5. La clase de la puerta
6. _____
7. _____
8. _____
9. _____
10. _____

D Now, write down how many of each of the items you listed in exercise C you can find in your classroom. Follow the model.

el pupitre: *Hay veintiséis pupitres.*

1. Hay una television.
2. Hay dos mesas.
3. Hay dos ventanas
4. Hay dos pizarras
5. Hay una puerta

E Look at the following numbers and see if you can figure out what comes next in each sequence. Follow the model.

dos, cuatro, seis, *ocho*

1. cero, diez, veinte, _____

2. veintiocho, veintiuno, catorce, _____ , _____

3. tres, seis, doce, _____

4. cinco, diez, quince, _____ , _____

5. dos, cuatro, _____ , dieciséis

F Many words in English come from Spanish. Count the number of objects in each row and write the numbers in the spaces. Then arrange the letters in the circles to form an "eventful" word.

t r e s   s i e t e

o c h o   c u a t r o

d o s

Let's go to the _r_ _o_ _d_ _e_ _o_ !

G Your Spanish teacher wants to get to know you better. You can help by filling out the following form with all of the necessary information.

La fecha de hoy es el _____ de _____ de _____ .

Me llamo _Vannet Pun_____ .

Soy de _____ .

Tengo __14__ años.

Mi número de teléfono es _____ .

3

El Primer Paso

Fecha _____

H Choose two of the people pictured here. Imagine that they are meeting for the first time. Write down the conversation that might take place.

You should probably start by having them say hello and introducing themselves. Use the information given below the pictures to write other questions and answers.

la señora García, profesora, Chile

Federico Ríos, estudiante, México

el señor Fernández, profesor, Puerto Rico

Dolores del Valle, estudiante, Estados Unidos

A: _____

B: _____

A: _____

B: _____

A: _____

B: _____

A: _____

B: _____

CAPÍTULO 1

Fecha _____

A Complete the following crossword puzzle according to the pictures below.

HORIZONTALES (Across)

2.

7.

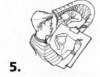

5.

8.

6.

10.

VERTICALES (Down)

1.

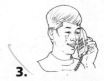

3.

4.

9.

B Susana, Andrés, and Eduardo are talking about what they like and what they don't like to do. Read their conversation to see what each one's preferences are.

¡¡¡SÁBADO ESPECTACULAR!!!

¿Te gusta escuchar música?

¿Y tocar la guitarra?

Si te gusta mucho practicar deportes...

Y también te gusta estar con amigos...

Si eres deportista y sociable...

VEN A SÁBADO ESPECTACULAR

en el gimnasio de la

Escuela Secundaria Benito Juárez

Sábado a las 6:00 P.M.

SUSANA   A mí no me gusta ver la tele, pero me gusta hablar por teléfono.

ANDRÉS   ¿De veras? Pues, a mí también me gusta, pero me gusta más practicar deportes. Y a ti, Eduardo, ¿qué te gusta más, practicar deportes o hablar por teléfono?

EDUARDO   Pues, a mí no me gusta practicar deportes. No me gusta hablar por teléfono tampoco, pero sí me gusta leer y estudiar.

Now tell whose likes and dislikes are most similar to your own, and explain why.

_____

_____

_____

CAPÍTULO 1

C Use the adjectives below to describe some of your classmates. Follow the model.

amable	callado(a)	generoso(a)	ordenado(a)	serio(a)
artístico(a)	deportista	gracioso(a)	paciente	sociable
atrevido(a)	desordenado(a)	impaciente	prudente	trabajador(a)

Juan (no) es muy paciente.

1. _____ es _____ .

2. _____ es _____ .

3. _____ es _____ .

4. _____ es _____ .

5. _____ es _____ .

6. _____ es _____ .

D Now, compare yourself to your classmates and describe what you are or are not like. Follow the model.

Yo soy paciente también. or: *Yo no soy paciente tampoco.*

1. _____ .

2. _____ .

3. _____ .

4. _____ .

5. _____ .

6. _____ .

E First look at the pictures and identify the activities. Then, tell what the person doing each activity is like. Follow the models.

Sara   *tocar la guitarra*

Pepe

Andrés

1. _____   3. _____

Carlos

Marta

2. _____   4. _____

Sara no es artística.

1. _____

2. _____

3. _____

4. _____

Now, see whether or not you share the same personality traits. Follow the model.

Yo soy deportista también. or: *Yo no soy deportista tampoco.*

1. _____

2. _____

3. _____

4. _____

F A reporter for the school newspaper has asked you and several other students in your classroom to submit an article for the paper. The article deals with personality traits and activities people like and dislike.

Before you begin writing, you might want to think about your own personality. In your article, use four adjectives that describe what you're like and four that describe what you're not like. Use *Soy...* and *No soy....* Then write down four things that you like to do and four things that you don't like to do. Use *Me gusta...* and *No me gusta....*

Once you finish writing, read your article and check to make sure that the words are spelled correctly. Did you use accent marks where necessary?

Now, write your article.

_____

_____

_____

_____

_____

_____

_____

_____

_____

_____

_____

_____

_____

_____

_____

_____

_____

_____

_____

G Two exchange students wrote you letters explaining what they like and don't like to do. Based on the letters, list the activities each student likes to do.

> ¡Hola! Me llamo Andrés. A mí me gusta practicar deportes. Me gusta nadar, pero me gusta más patinar. No me gusta nada ir al cine. No me gusta ayudar en casa tampoco. Soy muy sociable y amable, y me gusta mucho estar con amigos.

Things Andrés likes to do:

_____

_____

_____

_____

> ¡Hola! Me llamo Cristina. Me gusta mucho ir al cine, dibujar y tocar la guitarra. Me gusta mucho escuchar música también. No me gusta ni patinar ni nadar. No me gusta hablar por teléfono tampoco. Soy callada y prudente.

Things Cristina likes to do:

_____

_____

_____

_____

Now, choose the exchange student you would prefer to write to and explain why.

Me gusta más escribir a _____ .

A mí (no) me gusta _____ también/tampoco.

Nombre

Fecha

A Take a look at Luisa's schedule. Choose five of her classes and explain what school supplies she needs for each one. Follow the model.

Luisa necesita un cuaderno para la clase de español.

Primer semestre

1ª hora	español
2ª hora	música
3ª hora	inglés
4ª hora	educación física
5ª hora	almuerzo
6ª hora	ciencias sociales
7ª hora	matemáticas
8ª hora	ciencias

1. _____

2. _____

3. _____

4. _____

5. _____

Now, choose five classes that you are also taking and tell whether or not you need the same supplies. Follow the model.

Yo (no) necesito un cuaderno para la clase de español (también).

1. _____

2. _____

3. _____

4. _____

5. _____

B Think about the schedule you have now, and then imagine what your ideal schedule would be like. Do you prefer to have *(tener)* Spanish for first period or last period? When do you like to have lunch or physical education? Write down your top four choices for your ideal schedule. Follow the model.

A mí me gusta más tener educación física en la primera hora.

1. _____

2. _____

3. _____

4. _____

C When Isabel got home from school today, she found this note from her father about her brother,

> *¡Hola, Isabel! Tengo un problema. Roberto es muy desordenado. Él tiene muchas clases, pero no tiene ni cuadernos ni lápices. Tú eres más ordenada. Aquí está la lista de sus clases: español, geometría, arte, inglés, educación física y ciencias sociales. ¿Qué necesita Roberto para sus clases?*

Roberto.

What do you know about Isabel and Roberto?

Isabel es _____ .

Roberto es _____ .

Does Roberto have a lot of classes? How many?

_____

Based on your own personal experience, what do you think Roberto needs for his classes?

Roberto necesita _____

_____

_____

_____

_____

_____

D There is a new student at your school. You have been asked to help her get adjusted since you both have the same schedule. Write down for her when your classes begin and end. Follow the model.

La clase de español empieza a las ocho y termina a las ocho y cuarenta.

1. _____

2. _____

3. _____

4. _____

5. _____

E Ana Cristina and Fernando are comparing their schedules. Look at their schedules and answer the following questions.

COLEGIO DE EDUCACIÓN SUPERIOR
BOLETA DE EVALUACIÓN

Nombre	Año	Sexo
Fernando Gómez Torres	3°	M
	Asignatura	Semestre
Horario	Español	1°
8:00-8:45	Inglés	1°
8:55-9:40	Ciencias	1°
9:50-10:35	Matemáticas	1°
10:45-11:30	Educación física	1°
12:15-1:00	Ciencias sociales	1°
1:10-2:05		

COLEGIO DE EDUCACIÓN SUPERIOR
BOLETA DE EVALUACIÓN

Nombre	Año	Sexo
Ana Cristina López García	3°	F
	Asignatura	Semestre
Horario	Música	1°
8:00-8:45	Matemáticas	1°
8:55-9:40	Ciencias de la salud	1°
9:50-10:35	Inglés	1°
11:30-12:15	Educación física	1°
12:25-1:10	Español	1°
1:20-2:15		

1. ¿Cuándo empieza la clase de matemáticas de Fernando?

_____

2. ¿Es la clase de español de Ana Cristina a las ocho o a la una y veinte?

_____

3. ¿A qué hora termina la clase de inglés de Ana Cristina?

_____

4. ¿A qué hora termina la clase de ciencias de Fernando?

_____

5. Y tú, ¿tienes clase de educación física? ¿A qué hora empieza tu clase?

_____

Nombre ____________________

Fecha ____________________

Writing Activities

F Identify each of the following pictures by writing a sentence on the line provided. Follow the model.

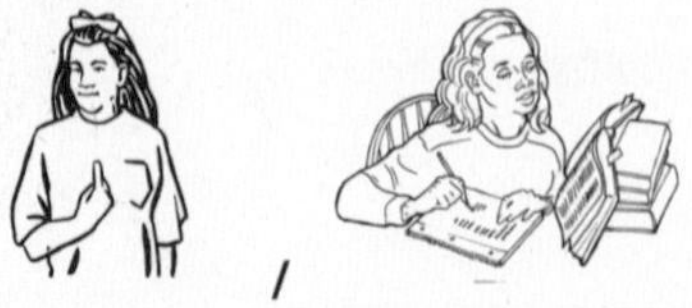

Yo estudio.

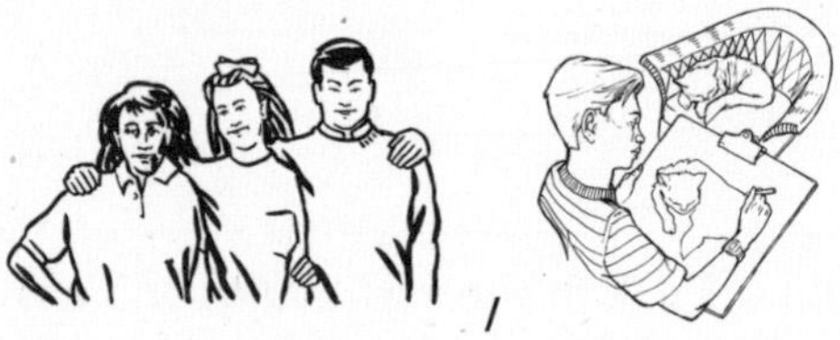

1. ______________________________

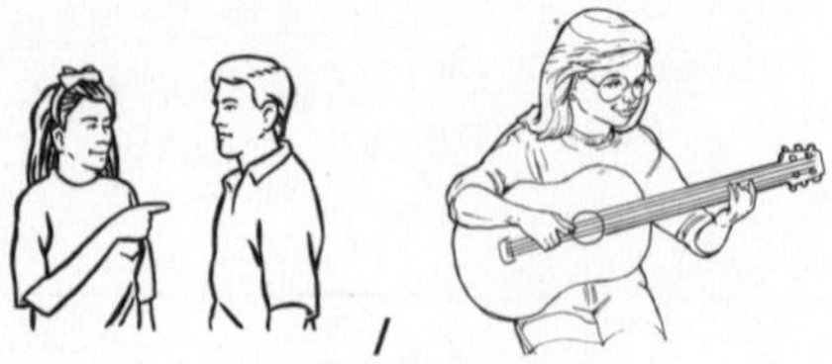

2. ______________________________

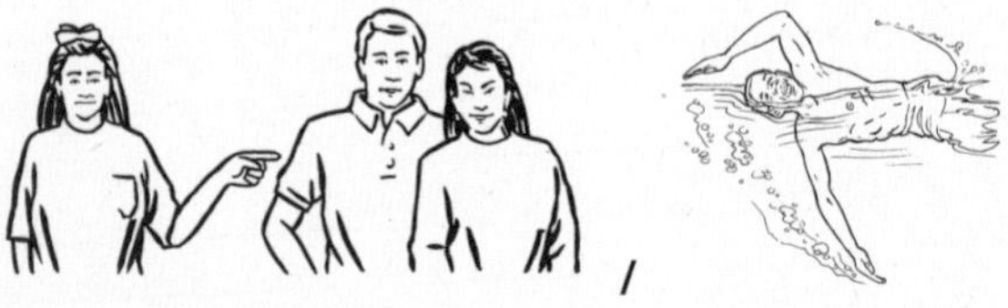

3. ______________________________

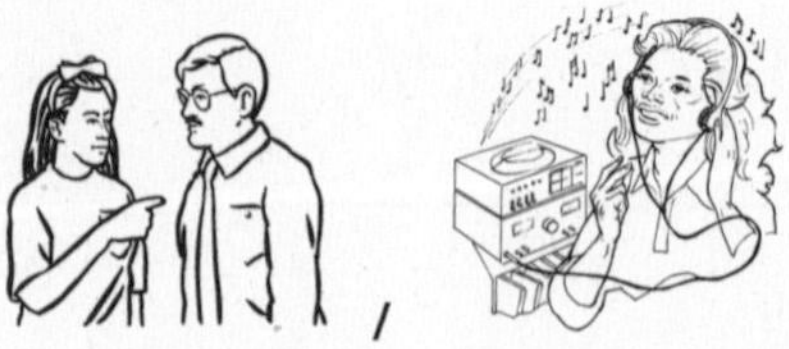

4. ______________________________

Now, write down at what time the person does each some of these activities.

2:00

Yo estudio a las dos.

1:45

1. _____

4:15

2. _____

9:20

3. _____

5:30

4. _____

G Pablo, an exchange student from Colombia, is going to be living with your family and going to school with you for the next year. You've already exchanged letters describing yourselves; now he has requested information about your school.

Before you begin writing, think about what you consider to be the most important things to tell someone about your school.

Make a list of the subjects you are studying. Use *tengo….* Write down two subjects that you like and two that you don't like. Use *me gusta…* and *no me gusta….* Indicate at what time your favorite class begins and ends. Use *empieza…* and *termina….* Also, make a list of the school supplies that you need for your classes. Use *necesito….*

Once you have finished writing, read your letter and check to make sure that all of the words are spelled correctly. Did you use accents where necessary?

Now, write your letter.

Hola, Pablo:

_____

_____

_____

_____

_____

_____

_____

_____

_____

_____

_____

_____

_____

_____

_____

_____

                              Saludos,

                              _____

A You are a very active young person and, therefore, your activities may vary from season to season. Name the activities that you enjoy doing in each of the four seasons. Follow the model.

En el invierno me gusta ir al cine. También me gusta practicar deportes en el gimnasio.

1. _____

   _____

2. _____

   _____

3. _____

   _____

4. _____

   _____

   _____

5. Which season do you prefer?

   A mí me gusta más _____

   _____

CAPÍTULO 3

Fecha

B Fill in the crossword puzzle with the correct Spanish word for each day of the week and each season of the year. Follow the clues in English.

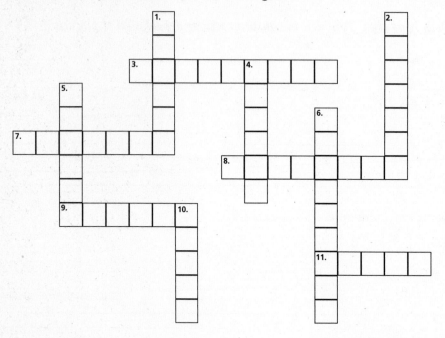

HORIZONTALES

3. When the weather is nice and school ends, it's…

7. Day between Thursday and Saturday

6. Day before Thursday

8. Brrr! It's cold and snowing!

9. Before Sunday comes…

11. First day of the week in Spanish

VERTICALES

1. After Monday comes…

2. Last day of the week in Spanish

4. Beach weather season!

5. Before Friday comes…

10. When leaves change colors and fall, it's…

C Think about the activities you usually do during the week. Choose five days of the week. Write down where you usually go on each day and give a reason. Follow the model.

Los lunes voy a la piscina. Me gusta nadar.

1. _____

2. _____

3. _____

4. _____

5. _____

D You are making plans for the weekend with your friends. Write down five questions to ask then about things you would like to do. Follow the model.

Me gustaría ir de pesca el sábado. ¿Y a ti? or: *¿Puedes jugar tenis conmigo mañana?*

1. _____

2. _____

3. _____

4. _____

5. _____

Now, write down their answers. Remember to use expressions like *¡Claro que sí!* and *¡Qué lástima!*

1. _____

2. _____

3. _____

4. _____

5. _____

E The boy in this picture, Pablo, is going to do some of his after-school activities.

From the way he is dressed, what season do you think it is?

_____

From the things he is carrying, where do you think he is going?

_____

Now, think about your own activities. Where are you going to go after school?

Después de las clases _____

_____

Pablo

CAPÍTULO 3

F Next week your school vacation begins!! Based on the pictures, write down what you and your classmates are going to do. Follow the model.

Marta   *Marta va a jugar béisbol.*

1. nosotros   _____

2. Juan y Maritza   _____

3. Sra. Méndez y Elena   _____

4. Carola   _____

5. yo   _____

G You're in the school cafeteria at lunchtime, but not everyone is eating. Based on the pictures, write down what each person is doing and with whom. Follow the model.

Mario /

Mario habla por teléfono con ella.

1. Tomás y yo /

_____

2. Luisita  /

_____

3. yo  /

_____

4. La Sra. Rodríguez /

_____

5. tú /

_____

H Today the teachers are holding conferences so there are no classes. Write three sentences telling where various members of your class are, and whether they are tired, busy, or ill. Use the verb *estar* and the adjectives *cansado, ocupado,* and *enfermo.* Don't forget to make the ending of each adjective agree with the gender of the person it is modifying. Follow the model.

Jorge   tired   *Jorge está en el parque de diversiones. Él está cansado.*

1. Pedro   busy   _____

2. Marta   sick   _____

3. Yo   tired   _____

I You're enjoying a vacation with your family in Puerto Rico, and you want to send a postcard to your friend Pablo to tell him about it.

Before you begin writing, think about the postcards that you've written or received in the past. What do you normally write about when you're on vacation?

Start by saying how you are. Use *Estoy....* Write down one place that you go to every day. Use *Voy....* Now, write down two activities that you have been doing. Use regular *-ar* verbs (for example: *nadar*) in the correct form. Now, write about two activities that you are going to do and when you are going to do them. Use *Voy a....*

Once you finish writing, read your postcard and check to make sure all the words are spelled correctly. Did you use accent marks where necessary?

Now, write your postcard.

Hola, Pablo:

_____   _____

_____   _____

_____   _____

_____   _____

_____   _____

A Look at the sandwich in the picture. Write a shopping list of the ingredients you might need to make this sandwich.

Ingredients:

_____

_____

_____

_____

_____

¿Te gusta el sandwich?

_____

porque _____.

B What do you prefer to eat for breakfast, lunch, and dinner? List two preferences for each meal. Follow the model.

Prefiero comer huevos en el desayuno.

Breakfast:

1. _____

2. _____

Lunch:

3. _____

4. _____

Dinner:

5. _____

6. _____

Now, write down what you like to drink for each meal. Follow the model.

Prefiero beber leche en el desayuno.

Breakfast:

1. _____

Lunch:

2. _____

Dinner:

3. _____

C See if you can find the names of these fifteen foods and beverages hidden in the word puzzle!
Circle the words that go across and down.

agua	huevos	café	fruta	lechuga
pescado	papas	leche	jamón	pan
plátanos	arroz	jugo	naranjas	limonada

A	L	P	L	A	T	A	N	O	S	O	P	U
K	Q	I	E	L	L	N	Y	B	C	A	F	E
A	U	F	C	U	P	A	P	A	S	I	R	A
L	E	C	H	E	O	R	S	C	E	T	U	H
E	S	P	U	J	E	A	R	R	O	Z	T	U
P	O	A	G	U	A	N	E	R	A	O	A	E
A	A	N	A	G	B	J	A	M	O	N	D	V
N	L	I	M	O	N	A	D	A	U	S	E	O
A	P	A	T	P	E	S	C	A	D	O	G	S

D You're going to have a party! Almost everything is organized; all you have to do now is to write the invitations.

Before you begin writing, think about the information that you should include in an invitation. First, write down the date of the party, then the hour, and finally the location where it will take place.

After writing the invitation, make a list of the things you are going to provide to eat and drink at the party. Use *Vamos a comer…* and *Vamos a beber….*

Once you finish writing, reread your invitation and check to make sure that all the words are spelled correctly. Include accents where necessary.

Now, write your invitation.

¡¡VAMOS A TENER UNA FIESTA!!

¿Cuándo? _____

a la(s) _____ de la tarde

¿Dónde? _____

_____

_____

_____

Now, write your list.

Lista de comidas y bebidas

Vamos a comer _____

_____

_____

_____

Vamos a beber _____

_____

_____

_____

E Ask four classmates about what foods they would like to have served at the school cafeteria. First, write your question, then write their answer on the line below it. Follow the model.

—*¿Te gustan los sandwiches?*

—*No, son horribles. Prefiero las ensaladas.* or: —*Sí, son sabrosos.*

1. —_____

—_____

2. —_____

—_____

3. —_____

—_____

4. —_____

—_____

5. —_____

—_____

F People like to watch what they eat these days. Look at the pictures and tell what each person is eating and whether it is good or bad for their health. Follow the model.

Juan   *Juan no come papas fritas. Son malas para la salud.*

1. Tú   _____

_____

2. Elena y Paco   _____

_____

3. Yo   _____

_____

4. Isabel y yo   _____

_____

G An article in the school newspaper talks about what some of your classmates like to eat and drink at each meal. Look at the pictures and state each one's preferences. Follow the model.

Marcos y Patricio /

Marcos y Patricio beben jugo de naranja en el desayuno.

1. Juan y Luisita /

_____

2. Jorge y yo /

_____

3. Leonor y Marta /

_____

4. Pepe y tú /

_____

5. Enrique /

_____

H Your friends are all very busy today. Write down where each one is and what he or she is doing there. Follow the model.

Ana y Carmela _____ / _____

Ana y Carmela están en el campo. Ana y Carmela tocan la guitarra.

1. Tomás y Pablo _____ / _____

_____

2. Isabel y Cristina _____ / _____

_____

3. Carlos y Alfredo _____ / _____

_____

4. José y yo _____ / _____

_____

5. Antonio y Ud. _____ / _____

_____

A You're planning a party for your family. Before you decide what you're going to prepare to eat, make a list of something that each member of your family likes or loves to eat as well as something that each one does not like. Follow the model.

A mi prima Alicia le encantan las zanahorias.

A mi prima Alicia no le gusta el pescado.

1. _____

   _____

2. _____

   _____

3. _____

   _____

4. _____

   _____

5. _____

   _____

Based on the above information, what are you going to eat at the party?

Vamos a comer _____

_____

_____

_____

_____

_____

_____

_____

_____

_____

B You need to provide the ages of some of your friends' relatives for a math project you are doing. Based on the information provided, write out complete sentences on the lines below. Follow the model.

Inés' mother / 47

La madre de Inés tiene cuarenta y siete años.

1. Bernardo's grandfather / 82

_____

_____

2. Ana María's uncle / 39

_____

_____

3. Julio's father / 54

_____

_____

4. Rosa's grandmother / 75

_____

_____

5. Alejandro's aunt / 42

_____

_____

CAPÍTULO 5   Fecha

C A good friend of yours is going to join you for the family party you planned in exercise A. Before the party starts, your friend has asked you to describe some of your relatives so that he will be able to identify them when they arrive. Choose five members of your family and describe them to your friend. Follow the model.

Mi prima Alicia es joven, baja y tiene los ojos azules.

1. _____
2. _____
3. _____
4. _____
5. _____

D Fill in the blanks with the appropriate words. Then, unscramble the circled letters to finish the statement below.

1. Mis dos hermanas Cristina y Luisa tienen cinco años. Ellas son ⊖ _ _ ⊖ _ _ _ .

2. La piscina no es grande. Es _ _ _ _ ⊖ _ .

3. Marcos no tiene hermanos. Él es hijo _ _ ⊖ _ .

4. El padre de mi padre es mi _ _ _ _ ⊖ _ .

5. La hija de mi tío es mi _ _ ⊖ _ .

6. Mi perro no es feo. Es _ _ _ ⊖ _ ⊖ _ .

7. Mis tíos no son viejos. Ellos son _ _ _ _ _ ⊖ _ .

8. Mi madre no es baja. Ella es _ _ ⊖ _ .

9. Mi tía no tiene gatos. Ella tiene _ ⊖ _ _ _ ⊖ .

¿Cómo son los estudiantes de la clase de español?

¡Ellos son __ __ __ __ __ __ __ __ __ __ __ !

CAPÍTULO 5   Fecha _____

E Your pen pal Juan Carlos, who is from Buenos Aires, Argentina, has asked you to tell him about a member of your family.

First, tell him the person's names. Use *Se llama....* Next, tell him the person's age. Use *Tiene...años.* Then, pick one adjective to describe the person physically *(alto, guapo)* and one adjective to describe his or her personality *(atrevido, prudente)*. Use *Es....* Don't forget to tell him about yourself and how old you are. Use *Tengo...años.* Finally, use two adjectives to describe yourself. Use *Soy....*

Once you finish writing, read your description and check to make sure that all the words are spelled correctly and that you have used accents where necessary. Also, check to make sure the endings of the adjectives agree with the nouns they are describing.

Now, write your letter to your pen pal.

Hola, Juan Carlos:

_____

_____

_____

_____

_____

_____

_____

_____

_____

_____

_____

_____

_____

_____

_____

_____

_____

Saludos,

_____

F Look at the picture of Eugenia's family. Does Eugenia have any brothers or sisters? Do you think her parents are young or old? How old do you think her mother is? And her father?

Eugenia

"Eugenia y su familia"

_____

_____

_____

_____

_____

Now think about your own family. Do you have any brothers or sisters? How many? Describe one of them. If you don't have any brothers or sisters, describe any other member of your family.

_____

_____

_____

_____

_____

G Look at the pictures and describe what the people are like and where they are going. Follow the model.

Gonzalo /

Gonzalo es atrevido. Él va al parque de diversiones.

1. nosotros / _____

2. Elena y Pilar / _____

3. tú / _____

4. yo / _____

H Look at the pictures and write down which classes these people are taking and what materials they need for each class. Follow the model.

Lourdes / *Lourdes tiene la clase de matemáticas. Ella necesita su calculadora.*

1. tú / _____
_____

2. yo / _____
_____

3. Gustavo / _____

A Fill in the puzzle according to the pictures.

HORIZONTALES

2.

5.

8.

11.

12.

VERTICALES

1.

3.

4.

6.

7.

9.

10.

35

B Read the advertisement below and then use it as a basis for writing a conversation between a customer and a salesperson. The salesperson should start by asking if the customer needs help. The customer in turn asks about the prices of different items of clothing. The conversation should end with the customer saying what he or she is going to buy.

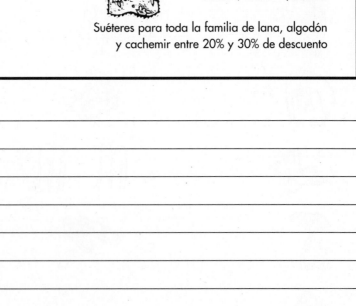

GRAN VENTA DE FIN DE AÑO
EN MODAS ÁLVAREZ
Oferta válida del 28 de diciembre al 5 de enero

PARA HOMBRES

Camisa de seda
Colores surtidos
Antes $54.95   **$45.00**

Pantalones
50% poliéster, 50% algodón
Colores: rojo, negro, blanco
Antes $37.45   **$28.50**

PARA MUJERES

Pantalones vaqueros
100% algodón
Antes $37.00   **$25.00**

Camiseta
Colores: rojo, negro, blanco
Tallas: P-M-G-SG
Antes $13.50   **$10.00**

Camisa franela de manga larga
Colores surtidos
Antes $25.00   **$19.95**

Vestidos de corte sencillo
Colores surtidos
Tallas: 6 a 18
Antes $49.99   **$35.00**

Suéteres para toda la familia de lana, algodón
y cachemir entre 20% y 30% de descuento

¡Y MUCHO MÁS!
Accesorios, zapatos,
medias, sombreros,
bufandas, guantes, botas,
chaquetas de cuero...

_____

_____

_____

_____

_____

_____

_____

_____

_____

_____

C Describe what you and four of your classmates are wearing today. Follow the model.

Yo llevo una falda roja y un suéter blanco.

1. _____

2. _____

3. _____

4. _____

5. _____

Now, write a description of your favorite outfit. Tell *where* and *when* you bought it and *how much* you paid for it. Follow the model.

Compré el vestido azul en el Almacén García hace un año. Pagué cuarenta dólares.

_____

_____

_____

_____

_____

_____

_____

_____

D Ana María is at the grocery store. Before she buys anything, she likes to know how much it costs. Based on the pictures, write five questions that she asks the grocer. Follow the model.

¿Cuánto cuestan estos plátanos?

1. _____

2. _____

3. _____

Now, write down the grocer's answers. Follow the model.

Esos plátanos cuestan dos dólares.

1. / $6 _____

2. / $1 _____

3. / $2 _____

E Look at the pictures and the information provided, then write a sentence which states when you bought each of the following items. Make sure to use the direct object pronouns: *lo, la, los, las.* Follow the model.

/ **1 week**   *Los compré hace una semana.*

1.   / **4 days**   _____

2.   / **2 months**   _____

3.   / **1 year**   _____

4.   / **3 weeks**   _____

F Look at the pictures and write two sentences which explain what each person needs and where he or she can look for it. Use the appropriate direct object pronouns: lo, la, los, las. Follow the model.

Paco   /

Paco necesita una camisa. La busca en una tienda de descuentos.

1. tú   /

_____

2. Elena   /

_____

3. Uds. _____ / _____

_____

G You are going away for a weekend to visit some friends. Before you begin packing, make a list of three items of clothing that you need to buy (use *Necesito comprar…*).

Make sure you say what color they are and where you're going to buy them. Use the correct direct object pronoun. Then, write down three things that you are going to do. Use *Voy a….* What clothes should you wear when you do these activities? Use *Debo llevar….*

Check to make sure that all of the words are spelled correctly, that you have used accents where necessary, and that the adjectives agree with the nouns they describe.

Now, write your list.

_____

_____

_____

_____

_____

_____

_____

_____

_____

_____

_____

A Unscramble the following sets of letters to form the names of places of interest. Then, unscramble the circled letters to find out what you can take home from those places of interest.

Ud. puede llevar ___ ___ ___   ___ ___ ___ ___ ___ ___ ___ ___ .

1. iidáempr

2. esuom

3. cldtraae

4. sttaaaacr

5. urnisa

6. ñoatamsn

B Look at these pictures from a travel brochure about Puerto Santiago, a town located on a very exciting island. Based on the pictures, make a list of all the activities that you can do there. Follow the model.

EN PUERTO SANTIAGO PUEDES:

Puedo comprar recuerdos.

_____

_____

_____

¿Por qué te gustaría ir a Puerto Santiago?

Quisiera visitar Puerto Santiago para _____

_____

_____

¿Qué lugares de interés te gustaría visitar en la isla? ¿Por qué?

_____

_____

C As the weather changes, so do the clothes that you should wear. Name one item of clothing that would be appropriate for each type of weather pictured. Follow the model.

Cuando hace frío, debo llevar una bufanda.

1. _____

2. _____

3. _____

4. _____

5. _____

Now, describe today's weather and what you're wearing. Then, write down what you are planning to wear tomorrow.

_____

_____

_____

_____

_____

_____

D You are on vacation in Costa Rica with a group of friends. Using the pictures, describe what things you can do there. Follow the model.

Pablo /   *Pablo puede explorar la selva.*

1. yo / _____

2. Marta y Tomás / _____

3. tú / _____

4. Carmen Gloria / _____

5. nosotros / _____

E Based on the pictures, write sentences which describe where each person is going in order to do a certain activity. Follow the model.

Tomás /   /   *Tomás va a la piscina para nadar.*

1. nosotros /   /

_____

2. Juan José /   /

_____

3. Luisa y Marta /   /

_____

4. yo /   /

_____

5. tú /   / ¿ ?

_____

CAPÍTULO 7

Fecha

F Based on the pictures below, write down what these people want to do on their next vacation and where they plan to go. Follow the model.

Javier / Puerto Rico

Javier quiere tomar el sol. Piensa ir a Puerto Rico.

1. Magdalena / las montañas /

_____

2. Jaime y yo / el lago

_____

3. Gerardo y Rafael / México

_____

4. Gloria y tú / el mar

_____

5. tú / San Francisco

_____

G Felipe is a very disorganized person. He is always searching for someone or something. Write sentences which describe who or what he is looking for. Don't forget to use the *a personal* when necessary. Follow the model.

Felipe / pasaporte

> *Felipe busca el pasaporte.*

1. Felipe / Diana

_____

2. Felipe / Óscar

_____

3. Felipe / bronceador

_____

4. Felipe / familia

_____

5. Felipe / bufanda

_____

H You've been asked to write an article for the school newspaper about a vacation you have taken. Before you begin writing, think about the places you visited and the different things you did.

First, tell your readers when you went to those places. Use *Yo fui....* Also tell them what the weather is like there and three things that you need to take with you when you go. Finally, describe three activities that you can do there. Use *Cuando tú vas a...puedes....*

Check to make sure that all the words are spelled correctly and that you have used accents where necessary. Did you use the appropriate forms of the verbs?

Now, write your article.

_____

_____

_____

_____

_____

_____

_____

_____

CAPÍTULO 8   Fecha

A Complete the following crossword puzzle according to the picture clues.

HORIZONTALES

5.

7.

8.

11.

12.

13.

14.

VERTICALES

1.

2.

3.

4.

6.

9.

10.

B Everyone in your family will be very busy today. Look at the pictures and write sentences which describe what they are going to do and where. Follow the model.

Mi hermano /   /

Mi hermano va a lavar la ropa en el lavadero.

1. Mi madre /   /

_____

2. Mis primos /   /

_____

3. Mi padre /   /

_____

4. Mi hermana /   /

_____

5. Mis tíos y yo /   /

_____

C In five separate sentences, list the items of furniture found in your bedroom. Include an adjective that describes the item in each sentence. Follow the model.

Hay una cama incómoda en mi dormitorio.

1. _____

_____

2. _____

_____

3. _____

_____

4. _____

_____

5. _____

_____

Now, write five sentences which list things what you don't have in your bedroom, but which you need. Follow the model.

No tengo un equipo de sonido, pero lo necesito.

1. _____

_____

2. _____

_____

3. _____

_____

4. _____

_____

5. _____

_____

D Together with some friends, you are getting everything organized for a party. Some are helping out by making the food. Look at the pictures and write down what each person is making. Follow the model.

Pilar /   *Pilar hace los sandwiches.*

1. Ricardo /

_____

2. Marisa y tú /

_____

3. yo /

_____

Other friends are helping by organizing the room and putting everything where it belongs. Look at the pictures and tell where they are putting each item. Follow the model.

Tomás /   *Tomás pone los sandwiches en la mesa.*

1. Teresa y Ud. /  /

_____

2. Alfonso / /

_____

3. yo / /

_____

E People don't always live where they would like to. The following people live near one place, but would rather be living somewhere else. Write sentences based on the pictures. Follow the model.

Sr. Rodríguez / _____ / _____

El señor Rodríguez vive cerca del museo, pero prefiere vivir cerca del parque.

1. tú / _____ / _____

_____

2. mis padres y yo / _____ / _____

_____

3. Uds. / _____ / _____

_____

F Look at the pictures and then state what each of the following people have to do today. Follow the model.

Nosotros /   *Tenemos que lavar nuestra ropa.*

1. Luisa /   _____

2. tú /   _____

3. Uds. /   _____

Now, write down two things you have to do today.

1. _____

2. _____

G You want to buy a house, but you have a limited budget. In order to fnd the right house, your real estate agent has asked you to make a list of what you're looking for.

First, list the rooms you need to have in your house. Use *Tengo que tener....* Next, list the rooms you prefer having. Use *Prefiero tener....* Finally, list the big pieces of furniture and appliances you have so that the real estate agent knows how much space you need. Use *Tengo....*

Check to make sure that all the words are spelled correctly. Did you use accents where necessary?

Now, write your list.

_____

_____

_____

_____

_____

_____

_____

_____

_____

H Imagine that you are going to rent either the apartment or the house described in these classified ads. Which one do you prefer? Choose one and list the furniture you will put in three rooms. What colors will they be? What will they be like?

APARTAMENTO Colonia Loma Linda, muy privado. Sin garaje. 3 dormitorios, 2 baños, sala, comedor y cocina. Con piscina y jardín. Patio amplio. Con vista del Parque Central. Cerca del museo y del supermercado.	**CASA ELEGANTE** Tipo colonial, 2 pisos, preciosa vista panorámica de la ciudad. Garaje para 2 carros, sala, comedor, cocina, 6 cuartos, 3 baños, patio interior. Lejos de la ciudad.

Prefiero _____ porque _____

_____ .

Los muebles para la casa/el apartamento.

Cuarto   Necesito:

_____   _____

_____   _____

_____   _____

Nombre _____

Fecha _____

A Find the words that refer to different parts of the body in the word puzzle below and match them to the corresponding clue. The clues will help you to discover them. The words may be horizontal, vertical or diagonal.

1. Las necesitas para subir la pirámide.   _____

2. La necesitas para pensar.   _____

3. Tienes cinco en cada mano.   _____

4. Los necesitas para ver la tele.   _____

5. La jirafa tiene uno muy grande.   _____

6. Llevas zapatos en los…   _____

7. Lo necesitas para escuchar música.   _____

8. Te duele cuando hablas demasiado.   _____

9. Cuando hace frío, llevas guantes en las…   _____

10. Cuando comes demasiado, te duele el…   _____

O	C	U	E	L	L	O	J	P
L	E	U	S	P	F	E	C	I
A	B	A	T	I	N	S	O	E
P	A	H	O	E	O	I	B	R
I	H	V	M	N	G	Z	E	N
E	P	N	A	A	U	Q	L	A
S	C	M	G	C	R	U	A	S
V	E	D	O	F	N	A	R	I
A	Z	L	S	I	C	D	U	G
R	G	A	R	G	A	N	T	A
I	D	J	S	D	B	E	O	S
S	O	E	U	E	E	L	S	E
M	J	Q	D	R	Z	S	G	T
Ñ	O	I	D	O	A	U	V	M
O	S	T	N	H	S	T	A	R

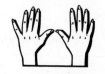

B Some of the students in your class don't feel very well today, so they have decided to go to the nurse's office. What might the nurse ask them if they told her that they had just...

1. practiced the guitar for three hours?

_____

2. cheered too much at a basketball game?

_____

3. run for two miles?

_____

4. eaten too much for lunch?

_____

5. read for six hours straight?

_____

Y a ti, ¿te duele algo? ¿Qué te duele?

_____

_____

C Look at the pictures, then write sentences which describe how these people are feeling today. Follow the model.

Paco /   *Paco tiene fiebre.*

1. Julia y Andrés /

_____

2. Fernando /

_____

3. Clara y tú /

_____

4. Claudia /

5. Ramón /

Now, make suggestions about what each of them should do in order to feel better. Follow the model.

Paco debe dormir.

1. _____

2. _____

3. _____

4. _____

5. _____

D You haven't been feeling well for quite some time now. In order to try to determine what is wrong with you, your doctor has asked you to keep a journal. You need to write today's entry.

Before you begin writing, think about how you feel. First, write down how long you have been feeling this way. Then, describe your symptoms. Where does it hurt?

Did you spell all the words correctly? Check to make sure that you have used the appropriate forms of the verbs.

Now, write your journal entry.

_____

_____

_____

_____

_____

_____

_____

_____

E Choose one of the doctors at the Clínica Familiar and one of the symptoms in the ad. What will the doctor ask you? How will you respond? Write your ideas in the form of a conversation. Include advice that the doctor might give you.

¿Tienes dolor de cabeza? ¿Dolor de espalda? ¿Dolor de estómago?
No tienes que vivir con dolores. Visita la **Clínica Familiar.**

Los médicos Sara Inés Melilla y Jorge Humberto Ríos te ofrecen servicios completos y profesionales.

Ven a la **Clínica Familiar** si
- te duele la espalda después de hacer ejercicio.
- te duelen los pies o las piernas.
- no puedes dormir bien.
- tienes fiebre.

Nuestros amables médicos te atenderán. Llámalos hoy mismo.

El médico o la médica se llama _____ .

Tus síntomas: _____ .

DR(A).: _____ .

TÚ: _____ .

DR(A).: _____ .

TÚ: _____ .

DR(A).: _____ .

TÚ: _____ .

DR(A).: _____ .

F You have just returned from a transatlantic flight together with some friends. You are all so tired that you have decided to take naps. Write sentences telling how long you and your friends have been sleeping. Follow the model.

yo / 2 hours

Hace dos horas que duermo.

1. Carmen y Gloria / 5 hours

_____

2. Víctor / 15 minutes

_____

3. Uds. / 4 hours

_____

4. nosotros / 30 minutes

_____

5. tú / 8 hours

_____

G Using the pictures below, list the places that these people like or love to go to in their spare time. Follow the model.

Juan /   *A Juan le gusta / le encanta el parque de diversiones.*

1. Silvia /

_____

2. tú /

_____

3. Roberto /

_____

4. yo /

_____

_____

5. Alfredo /

_____

_____

H You're at a department store and they're having a great two-for-one sale. Rather than get two identical items, you would like each one to be a different color. Follow the model.

green / blue   *Quiero la blusa azul y la verde.*

1.   **purple / white**

_____

2.   **black / brown**

_____

3.   **orange / grey**

_____

4.   **pink / yellow**

_____

5.   **red / blue**

_____

A Look at the pictures, then write five sentences which tell where you have to go in order to run the following errands. Follow the model.

Tengo que ir al banco para depositar dinero.

1. _____

2. _____

3. _____

4. _____

B How much money did these people pay for the items they recently purchased for their homes? Write your answers in complete sentences. Follow the model.

Lola / / $248   *Lola pagó doscientos cuarenta y ocho dólares por la cama.*

1. yo / / $320

_____

2. mis padres y yo / / $780

_____

3. Tomás y Ricardo /   / $1,200

_____

4. tú /   / $800

_____

C Read the clues and then write the names of the following places.

1. Puedes dormir aquí, pero tienes que pagar dinero.

____ ____ ____ ____ ____

2. Aquí puedes comer y no tienes que lavar los platos después.

____ ____ ____ ____ ____ ____ ____ ____ ____ ____

3. Todos los coches van aquí cuando necesitan gasolina.

____ ____ ____ ____ ____ ____ ____

____ ____ ____ ____ ____ ____ ____ ____ ____

4. Cuando te duele la cabeza, vas aquí para comprar algo.

____ ____ ____ ____ ____ ____ ____

5. Aquí hay libros, pero no puedes comprarlos.

____ ____ ____ ____ ____ ____ ____ ____ ____

6. Vas aquí cuando quieres ver un partido de fútbol.

____ ____ ____ ____ ____ ____

7. Aquí puedes comprar libros.

____ ____ ____ ____ ____ ____ ____

8. Aquí viven muchos animales.

____ ____ ____ ____ ____ ____ ____ ____

D Your friend Lourdes is coming to visit your city. Using the map below tell her where the following places are located. Follow the model.

El teatro está en la avenida Sol, al lado del zoológico / a la derecha del zoológico.

1. _____

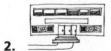

2. _____

3. _____

4. _____

E Everyone in your family was busy doing their chores yesterday. Look at the pictures and write down what each person did. Follow the model.

mi madre /   *Mi madre pasó la aspiradora.*

1. mi hermana / _____

2. yo / _____

3. mis hermanos / _____

4. mi padre / _____

5. mis abuelos / _____

F Look at the pictures and then explain how each of the following people got to school yesterday. Follow the model.

José /   *José fue a la escuela a pie ayer.*

1. nosotros / _____

2. yo / _____

3. tú / _____

4. Uds. / _____

5. Luisa / _____

CAPÍTULO 10

G Your friends Laura and Rosa have written to you to ask for advice about where to go on their vacation. Before you begin writing to them, think about a place that you visited last year.

Start your letter by suggesting where they should go. Use *Uds. deben ir....* Continue by explaining when you went there and with whom. Use *Fui a....* Now, tell them what you did while you were there. Use the *-ar* verbs that you know and the verb *ir* in the preterite tense. Finish your letter by telling them what they should take on their vacation. Use *Uds. deben llevar....*

Check to make sure that all of the words are spelled correctly. Did you use accents where necessary?

Now, write your letter.

Hola, Laura y Rosa:

_____

_____

_____

_____

_____

_____

_____

_____

_____

_____

_____

_____

_____

_____

_____

_____

_____

_____

_____

Saludos,

_____

H　Here's a map to help you get to the Museo de Artesanía Iberoamericana in La Orotava (Tenerife, Spain). Look at the map and then answer the questions.

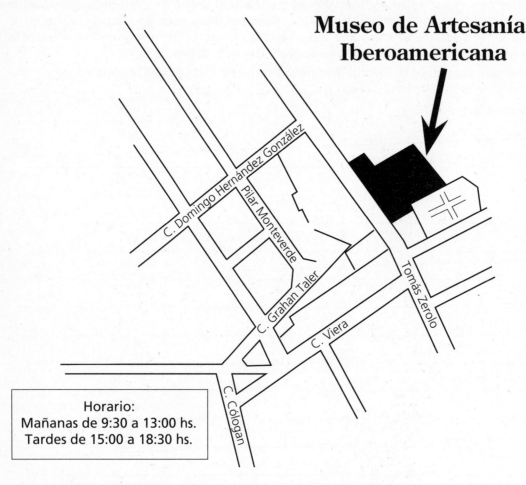

Museo de Artesanía Iberoamericana

Horario:
Mañanas de 9:30 a 13:00 hs.
Tardes de 15:00 a 18:30 hs.

1. ¿Dónde está el Museo de Artesanía Iberoamericana?

_____

2. ¿A qué hora va a abrir el museo por la mañana? ¿Y por la tarde?

_____

3. ¿A qué hora va a cerrar por la mañana?

_____

4. ¿A qué hora va a cerrar por la tarde?

_____

5. Si vas a ese museo, ¿qué crees que puedes ver o comprar allí?

_____

CAPÍTULO 11

Fecha

A Read the clues and look at the pictures below to complete this crossword puzzle.

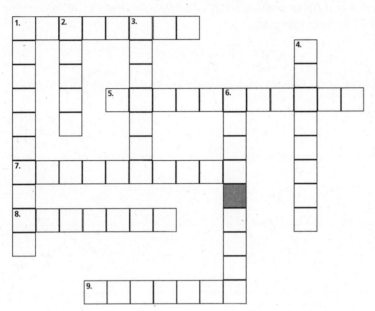

HORIZONTALES

1. ¿Cuál es tu _____ favorito?

5.

7.

8.

9.

VERTICALES

1. el _____ del tiempo

2.

3.

4.

6. el programa de hechos de la _____

B Look at each picture and choose the title of a movie or a television program that is associated with that category. Then, write complete sentences in which you name that program or movie and express your opinion of it. Follow the model.

Guys and Dolls *es una película musical. Me gusta mucho.*

1. _____

2. _____

3. _____

4. _____

C Some new students at your school have just received their schedules. Help them out by explaining how long each of their classes lasts and when it begins and ends. Follow the model.

ENGLISH TODAY

11:15 A.M. - 12:00 P.M.

La clase de inglés dura cuarenta y cinco minutos, de las once y quince de la mañana hasta las doce en punto de la tarde.

1. 8:35 A.M. - 9:20 A.M. _____

_____

2. 10:15 A.M. - 11:15 A.M. _____

_____

3. 11:30 A.M. -12:35 P.M. _____

_____

D Write comparisons in which you combine the following two sentences. Follow the model.

Tomás es alto. Marta es baja.

Marta es menos alta que Tomás. or: *Tomás es más alto que Marta.*

1. Arturo y Sonia son viejos. María Luisa es joven.

_____

2. La ensalada es buena para la salud. Las papas fritas son malas para la salud.

_____

3. Las comedias son interesantes. Los anuncios son aburridos.

_____

4. Mi dormitorio es pequeño. El dormitorio de mis padres es grande.

_____

E Here are the results of a survey about the saddest and the most interesting, amusing, boring, and exciting kinds of television programs. Write complete sentences that correspond to the pictures. Use the information provided. Follow the model.

/ interesante   *El programa de entrevistas es el programa más interesante.*

1. / divertido   _____

2. / aburrido   _____

3. / emocionante   _____

4. / triste   _____

F Look at the pictures and describe what each person saw on television last night. Then, say that you are going to watch the same program tomorrow. Follow the model.

Antonio /

Antonio vio las noticias anoche. Voy a verlas mañana.

or: *Las voy a ver mañana.*

1. Uds. /

_____

_____

2. tú /

_____

_____

3. Consuelo y María /

_____

_____

4. Ricardo /

_____

_____

G You and a friend agree about the kinds of films that interest, fascinate, and bore the both of you. Write complete sentences to express your opinions. Follow the model.

Nos interesan las películas de ciencia ficción.

1. _____

2. _____

3. _____

4. _____

H Your friend has lost his weekly television guide, so he has asked you to suggest something that he can watch tonight.

Start by saying the name of a program that is on television tonight. Don't forget to include the channel! Use *Dan... en el canal....* Continue by saying how long it lasts, what time it begins and when it ends. Use *Dura..., ...de la tarde, hasta....* Now, say what kind of program it is. Use *Es....* Also, say what you think about the program. Use *Pienso que es...* and the adjectives you know. Finally, give your reaction to the program. Does it interest, fascinate, or bore you? Why? Use *Me (interesa) porque....*

Check to make sure that the verbs and adjectives are in the correct form. Don't forget to check for accents and correct spelling.

Now, write your suggestion.

_____

_____

_____

_____

_____

_____

_____

_____

_____

_____

_____

_____

_____

_____

_____

_____

_____

I Look at the following page of the TV listings in a newspaper. What kinds of programs are being shown on August 12?

DOMINGO 12 de agosto

Tele-2

8:00 **Dibujos animados:** Daniel el travieso

8:30 **Cine infantil:** *El monstruo del Planeta X.* Un extraterrestre aterriza en la Tierra y hace amistad con un niño.

12:00 **Fiesta caribeña:** Música popular del Caribe.

TV-6

8:00 **El mundo de la ciencia:** Los delfines

9:30 **Fútbol vía satélite:** Campeonato de liga: Real Madrid vs. Valencia

1:00 **Cine en su casa:** *Robin Hood y los piratas.* Robin Hood, preso por piratas, se escapa y regresa al condado de Sherwood.

ANTENA-12

8:30 **Noticias al instante**

9:30 **Cine del oeste:** *Siete vaqueros de Río Diablo.* Unos vaqueros rescatan un pueblo, aterrorizado por bandidos.

11:30 **Comedia:** *La familia Loca.* La familia Loca va de vacaciones.

12:00 **Entre nosotros:** Cecilia Bucólica entrevista a cantantes, actores y políticos.

Clase de programa   **Nombre del programa**

Dibujos animados   _____

Película de ciencia ficción   _____

Programa musical   _____

Programa educativo   _____

Programa de deportes   _____

Película de aventuras   _____

Noticias   _____

Película del oeste   _____

Comedia   _____

Programa de entrevistas   _____

¿Qué programa vas a ver? ¿Por qué te interesa?

Voy a ver _____

Me interesa porque _____

_____

_____

_____

_____

A Look at the pictures and then complete the crossword puzzle.

HORIZONTALES

6.

8.

9.

11.

12.

13.

16.

17.

VERTICALES

1.

2.

3.

4.

5.

7.

10.

14.

B Name some Mexican dishes that you have tried. Then, say what ingredients are used to make them. Follow the model.

He probado los tacos. Son de tortillas de maíz con pollo o carne de res.

1. _____
2. _____
3. _____
4. _____
5. _____

C Marcos's little brother wants to help him set the table. Look at each picture, then tell him where the item should be placed. Follow the model.

El cuchillo debe estar a la derecha del plato.

1. _____

2. _____

3. _____

4. _____

CAPÍTULO 12

Fecha _____

D The following people have ordered a particular dish, but since the waiter is new and a bit confused he serves them something else. Look at the pictures and then write sentences which describe what's happening. Follow the model.

Carlos   /   *Carlos pide helado, pero el camarero le sirve flan.*

1. Juanito y yo   /   _____

_____

2. Uds.   /   _____

_____

3. tú   /   _____

_____

4. yo   /   _____

_____

E These people are sick in bed today. Look at the pictures and then write down what you're bringing to help cheer them up. Follow the model.

mi hermano /   *Le traigo un cuaderno a mi hermano.*

1. mis abuelos /   _____

2. tú /   _____

3. mi amigo /   _____

4. Elsa y Lola /   _____

F You went to a party last night with a friend, but he left early. Now he wants to know what time some of the other guests left. Give him this information in the form of complete sentences. Follow the model.

María / 10:30   *María salió a las diez y media.*

1. Juan y Paco / 10:45   _____

_____

2. Carolina / 11:05   _____

_____

3. Ricardo y yo / 11:15   _____

_____

Now, tell him what you and some of the other guests ate or drank after he left. Follow the model.

Lourdes /   *Lourdes bebió café.*

1. Marta /   _____

2. yo /   _____

3. Carlos y Tomás /   _____

CAPÍTULO 12   Fecha

G You're on vacation in Acapulco, Mexico, and you want to send a postcard to Manolo, your best friend at home.

Start by asking your friend how he is and telling him how you are. Use *¿Cómo estás? Yo estoy....* Tell your friend what the weather is like. Use the weather expressions with *Hace....* Now, tell him what you did yesterday and the day before. Use the preterite of the verbs you know, such as *ir, ver, comer,* or *salir.* Don't forget to tell him some of the new foods you have tried while in Mexico. Use *He probado....* Also, tell him what ingredients are used to make these dishes. Use *Es/Son de....* Don't forget to say if you liked them or not. Use *(No) Me gustó/gustaron....*

Check your work for correct spelling and accents, particularly in the preterite verb forms.

Now, write your postcard.

¡Hola, Manolo!:

_____

_____

_____

_____

_____

_____

_____

_____

_____

_____

_____

¡Hasta pronto!

_____

H Look at this picture of Marcos and Isabel eating Sunday breakfast in a restaurant. What do you think they might be talking about? Write a conversation for them.

They might ask each other what they ordered and/or if they've ever tried that dish before. Maybe one will ask the other if he or she wants to try it. After someone tries something, you usually ask if he or she likes it. They will also probably ask to have something passed to them, like the butter, salt, or pepper, or the milk or sugar for their coffee. Don't forget to include "please" and "thank you" where appropriate.

ISABEL: _____ .

MARCOS: _____ .

ISABEL: _____ .

MARCOS: _____ .

ISABEL: _____ .

MARCOS: _____ .

ISABEL: _____ .

MARCOS: _____ .

What do you usually order when you go to a restaurant for breakfast?

Pido _____ cuando voy a un restaurante para desayunar.

CAPÍTULO 13   Fecha

Think of six things that should or should not be done if we wish to preserve all living things. Write complete sentences, following the model.

Hay que limpiar el agua contaminada.

1. _____ .
2. _____ .
3. _____ .
4. _____ .
5. _____ .
6. _____ .

D Your family is having a reunion and you're standing next to your grandfather, who doesn't hear very well. Listen to what each person is saying and then repeat it for your grandfather. Follow the model.

Elena: "Estoy muy cansada."   *Elena dice que está muy cansada.*

1. Mi madre y mi abuela: "Hace mucho calor aquí."

_____

2. Mi padre: "Voy a abrir una ventana."

_____

3. Raúl: "Los pasteles son muy sabrosos."

_____

4. Yo: "No he probado los pasteles."

_____

5. Mi primo y yo: "Vamos a probarlos."

_____

6. Usted y María: "La salsa está muy picante."

_____

E You're organizing an environmental club at your school, and some of your friends have come to help. Look at the pictures and then give each one a job to do. Follow the model.

reciclar /   *Recicla los periódicos.*

1. separar / _____

2. sacar / _____

3. hacer / _____

4. apagar / _____

F The following people are applying for jobs at a summer camp which require certain skills. Look at the pictures and then write down what each person knows how to do. Follow the model.

Uds. /   *Uds. saben nadar.*

1. yo / _____

2. Juanito / _____

3. nosotros / _____

4. tú / _____

CAPÍTULO 13   Fecha

G You're planning a dinner party, but you won't be able to complete all the preparations in time. Your younger brother has offered to help by making a vegetable tray for you. Since this is the first time he has prepared such a tray, you need to write detailed instructions for him.

First, make a list of ingredients. Your tray might include lettuce, carrots, tomatoes, onions, or anything else you prefer. Next, tell him to wash *(lavar)* the lettuce. Use *el mandato afirmativo (tú)* of all the verbs in the instructions. Now, tell him to separate *(separar)* the lettuce and put *(poner)* it on a plate. Don't forget that *poner* has an irregular form! Next, tell him to wash and cut *(cortar)* each one of the other ingredients for the tray. Finally, tell him to make (*hacer* also has an irregular form!) sauces for the vegetables.

Check to make sure that the verb forms are correct. Also, check for correct spelling and accents. Finally, did you put all object pronouns in the right place?

Now, write your instructions.

Ingredientes: **Instrucciones:**

_____   _____

_____   _____

_____   _____

_____   _____

_____   _____

_____   _____

_____   _____

_____   _____

_____   _____

_____   _____

_____   _____

H Look at the poster and then answer the question below. Follow the model.

LUIS EL LOBO DICE...

Usa los senderos. No debemos destruir ni las flores ni las plantas.

Pide permiso a un guarda forestal si quieres encender un fuego.

Apaga el fuego antes de salir del campamento.

Al salir del bosque, lleva contigo toda la basura.

Pon la basura en un basurero y tápalo.

Proteje el bosque. Muchas personas van a visitarlo este año.

YO SÉ QUE PODEMOS
PROTEGER Y CUIDAR EL BOSQUE CON TU AYUDA.

¿Qué hacen estas personas para proteger el medio ambiente?   *Usan los senderos.*

¿Qué más pueden hacer ellos y otras personas para proteger los bosques?

_____

_____

_____

_____

_____

_____

_____

_____

A Unscramble the words below to discover all of the things you need to make your party a success! Then, unscramble the circled letters to find out what kind of party it is.

1. tinciiovnsae ____ ____ ____ ____ ____ ____ (○) ____ ____ ____

2. lgosrea (○) ____ ____ ____ ____ ____ ____

3. eelaptss (○) ____ ____ ____ ____ ____

4. msaciú ____ (○) ____ ____ ____

5. vitiandos ____ ____ ____ (○) ____ ____ ____

6. coroinedeasc ____ ____ ____ ____ ____ ____ (○) ____

7. eiabl ____ ____ (○) ____

8. frroscees ____ ____ (○) ____ ____ ____

¿Qué tipo de fiesta es? ____ ____ ____ ____ ____ ____ ____ ____

B What types of presents do your relatives and friends usually give you for your birthday? Follow the model.

tu hermano　　　*Mi hermano suele darme un regalo hecho a mano.*

1. tus padres _____

2. tus parientes _____

3. tu mejor amigo(a) _____

4. tu novio(a) _____

5. tus hermanos _____

6. tu primo _____

7. tu prima _____

8. tus abuelos _____

C Think about the last party you attended. What did you wear? Follow the model.

Yo llevé un vestido, zapatos de tacón alto, aretes y un collar.

_____

_____

_____

What did some of the other guests wear? Follow the model.

Raúl llevó un traje azul y un reloj pulsera muy elegante.

1. _____

_____

2. _____

_____

3. _____

_____

D You have agreed to complete a questionnaire for your favorite clothing store. However, the questions are so outrageous that you answer all of them negatively. Follow the model.

¿Cuándo llevas zapatos de tacón alto con un traje de baño?

Nunca llevo zapatos de tacón alto con un traje de baño.

1. ¿Llevas zapatos o tenis en la piscina?

_____

2. ¿Quién te compra cuarenta vestidos de fiesta?

_____

3. ¿Te gusta dormir con una corbata? ¿Te gusta dormir con un abrigo?

_____

4. ¿Cuándo llevas tres relojes pulsera?

_____

5. ¿Compras algo cuando no tienes dinero?

_____

E You're having a party and it seems to be a big success. Look at the pictures and then write down what each person is doing right now. Follow the model.

Tomás y Pablo / comer /   *Tomás y Pablo están comiendo sandwiches.*

1. muchos invitados / _____

2. tú / _____

3. Ricardo / beber / _____

4. Marta y yo / _____

5. yo / _____

F At this moment, you're writing the answers to this exercise. What are the other members of your family doing right now? Follow the model.

Mi madre está trabajando en la tienda de música.

1. _____

2. _____

3. _____

4. _____

5. _____

CAPÍTULO 14

G Your friend María is having a party for her fifteenth birthday, and you can't wait to find out what gifts she receives. Look at the pictures, and then write complete sentences describing what each person is giving her. Follow the model.

Luisa /   *Luisa le da anteojos de sol.*

1. sus padres / _____

2. su novio / _____

3. sus tíos / _____

4. tú / _____

5. yo / _____

6. nosotros / _____

CAPÍTULO 14   Fecha

H Recently it was your birthday and you received many wonderful presents. Now it's time to write some thank-you notes. Decide which gift you want to start with, and then think about what is important to say in a thank-you note.

Start by saying thank you for the gift. Use *Muchas gracias por....* Describe the gift. Use *Es....* Continue by saying that you like the gift a lot; don't forget to say why. Use *Me gusta(n) mucho... porque....* It's also nice to include a sentence about when you used the gift, if you already have, or when you're going to use it, if you haven't yet done so. Use the appropriate verb either in the preterite or in the immediate future *(Voy a...).* End your thank-you note with a brief closing.

Check your note for correct spelling and accents. Make sure your adjectives agree. Also, don't forget to check your verb forms.

Now, write your thank-you note.

Querido(a) _____ :

_____

_____

_____

_____

_____

_____

_____

_____

_____

_____

_____

Un abrazo,

_____

I Read these ads from the social page of the local newspaper. Then, answer the following questions.

Vida social **¡Don Francisco Eduardo Quintanilla** **cumple 100 años!** Entre los besos y abrazos de su familia, don Francisco Eduardo Quintanilla va a cumplir 100 años el 6 de agosto. La fiesta va a ser una celebración entre familia.	**Felicitaciones** La señorita Mireya Rosita Azuela Ibarra va a recibir su diploma de Bachiller en Computación del Instituto Tecnológico Comercial. Después de la ceremonia, va a celebrar con sus amigos y parientes en el restaurante Cuatro Caminos.
Fiesta infantil Con motivo de celebrar su 6° cumpleaños, la familia de Lidia Cervantes Alvarado va a hacer una simpática fiesta de cumpleaños. Dice Lidia: "Me encantan mis amigos, pero me encantan más los regalos."	**Humberto Alejandro Orellana López celebra** **su feliz cumpleaños... ¡en el campo!** El feliz día de su cumpleaños, Humberto Alejandro Orellana López, hijo de don Ricardo Orellana Buendía y doña Leticia López de Orellana, va a dar una fiesta en el Parque Municipal. "Siempre he deseado una fiesta de cumpleaños en la que los invitados pueden escuchar música, bailar al aire libre, practicar deportes, nadar y comer bien," nos comentó Humberto.

¿Quién no va a tener una fiesta de cumpleaños? ¿Por qué?

_____

_____

¿Vas a llevar un traje o un vestido largo a la fiesta de Humberto Alejandro Orellana López? ¿Por qué?

_____

_____

¿A qué fiesta te gustaría ir? ¿Por qué?

_____

_____

¿Qué vas a llevar a la fiesta?

_____

_____

Audio Activities

EL PRIMER PASO

Fecha

Actividad P.1

You're at a party with students visiting from Mexico. You have memorized several responses to things they might say when you meet them. Listen to each question or statement and write the letter of the best response in the blank. You will hear each question or statement twice.

a.	Me llamo . . .
b.	Muy bien, gracias.
c.	Soy de . . .
d.	Mucho gusto.

1.	
2.	
3.	
4.	
5.	
6.	

Actividad P.2

Your teacher is using an approximated map and an alphabet/number grid to plan a class trip to Spain. The five dots on the grid represent cities in Spain where your group will stop. Listen as you hear the first letter / number combination, as in a game of Bingo. Find that dot on the grid and label it "1." Next to it, write the name of the city. After you hear the second letter / number combination, find the second dot and label it "2," writing the name of the city next to it, and so on for the rest of the dots. Connect the dots to show the route of the class trip.

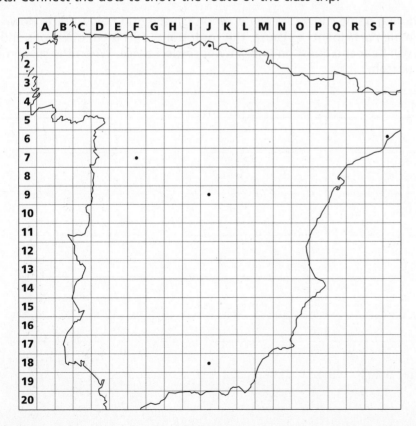

91

Nombre _____

EL PRIMER PASO

Fecha _____

Actividad P.3

While visiting in Guatemala, you happen to walk by a playground where children are playing a game in which they tell their name and date of birth. Write the name of the child beside the corresponding date of birth.

2 de diciembre   _____

25 de septiembre   _____

19 de mayo   _____

25 de junio   _____

30 de octubre   _____

13 de marzo   _____

31 de enero   _____

20 de julio   _____

Actividad P.4

Listen to the contestants on the dating game show *Cita con el amor*. On the grid below, write down the information about the three male participants as Laura, the contestant, asks them questions and ultimately chooses her date. You will hear the question-and-answer session twice. When the session is over, answer the question at the bottom.

	1.	2.	3.
Nombre	_____	_____	_____
País	_____	_____	_____
Profesión	_____	_____	_____
Edad	_____	_____	_____
Cumpleaños	_____	_____	_____

Whom did Laura choose as her date? _____

Actividad 1.1

You can find out a lot about a person by what he or she likes to do. You will hear two people from each group describe themselves. Listen and match the descriptions to the appropriate pictures. Put a "1" next to the first person described, and a "2" next to the second person described. You will hear each set of statements twice.

1. Luisa
_____

Marta
_____

Carmen
_____

2. Marco
_____

Javier
_____

Alejandro
_____

3. Mercedes
_____

Ana
_____

María
_____

4. Carlos
_____

Jaime
_____

Luis
_____

5. Carmen
_____

Margarita
_____

Cristina
_____

Actividad 1.2

Your teacher has asked each student in your class to find the ideal partner to work with for the day. The partners should be as alike as possible. Listen to the following questions and answer aloud in the pause after each question. Be sure to answer truthfully so you can be paired with the ideal partner. Your teacher will record the answers to help sort out the pairs. You will hear each question twice.

Actividad 1.3

Five of your friends in Spanish class are going to send an exchange tape to a group of students in Spain. Listen as each person says his or her name, tells about a favorite thing to do, and mentions a personality trait. Write each person's name under the corresponding picture. You will hear each statement twice.

1. Nombre: _____

2. Nombre: _____

3. Nombre: _____

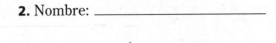

4. Nombre: _____

5. Nombre: _____

CAPÍTULO 1

Actividad 1.4

As a volunteer for a voice mail dating service at your school, you need to listen to recorded messages of people describing themselves. Your job is to find at least **three** things each person has in common with another. Listen and put a check mark in the appropriate boxes. Then, write the names of the ideal couples below the grid. You will hear each description twice.

	Susana	Pedro	Ana	Andrés	Laura	Luis
ver la televisión						
gracioso(a)						
sociable						
ir al cine						
ordenado(a)						
dibujar						
deportista						
escuchar música						
estar con amigos						
trabajador(a)						

Parejas ideales:

1. _____   2. _____   3. _____

Actividad 1.5

Radio talk show host Luisa is interviewing six mystery panelists. Luisa will call on them by number. As you listen, note down the answers in the corresponding boxes in the game grid. (In some cases the panelists give more than one clue in their answers.) You will hear the entire question-and-answer session repeated. At the end, you must correctly match up the three characteristics of each panelist with the biographical information given. Then write down the correct names of the panelists at the bottom of the grid. Check your answers against those provided on the tape at the end of the activity.

Número 1	Número 2	Número 3	Número 4	Número 5	Número 6
Nombre:	Nombre:	Nombre:	Nombre:	Nombre:	Nombre:

Actividad 2.1

You overhear several people in the hall trying to find out if they have any classes together this year. As you listen to each conversation, write an X in the box under *SÍ* if they have a class together, or under *NO* if they do not. You will hear each conversation twice.

	SÍ	NO
1.		
2.		
3.		
4.		
5.		

Actividad 2.2

As the summer receptionist at a resort in Mexico, you have to write down the wake-up call requests from the hotel guests. Listen to the messages left by six guests for tomorrow morning and fill in each person's room number and time requested for the wake-up call. You will hear each request twice.

	NÚMERO DE HABITACIÓN (Room number)	LA HORA DE DESPERTARSE (Wake-up time)
1.		
2.		
3.		
4.		
5.		
6.		

Actividad 2.3

A local store is offering a coupon for a free video rental for every five dollars spent on school supplies in their store. Listen to the sales clerk ringing up the items. On the receipt, write the amount spent for each item. Then add the total amount spent by each customer, and the number of free video coupons he or she will get. You will hear each statement twice.

1	2	3	4
$	$	$	$
$	$	$	$
$	$	$	$
$	$	$	$
$	$	$	$
$	$	$	$
$	$	$	$
TOTAL $	**TOTAL $**	**TOTAL $**	**TOTAL $**
CUPONES =	**CUPONES =**	**CUPONES =**	**CUPONES =**

Actividad 2.4

As one of the judges at your school's fall carnival, you mark on the master tic tac toe board the progress of a competition between the 10th graders (Team X) and the 11th graders (Team O). As each contestant comes to the microphone, you will hear *Para X* or *Para O* to indicate for which team he or she is playing, and then a description of the picture the contestant wants to play. You will hear each statement twice. At the end of this segment, see which grade won the game.

Actividad 2.5

As you stand by the school counselor's office, you hear four students requesting to get out of a certain class. From the part of the conversation you hear, write in the blank the class from which each student is requesting a transfer. You will hear each statement twice.

CLASE	PROFESOR O PROFESORA
1. matemáticas	**el profesor Pérez**
2. arte	**la profesora Muñoz**
3. español	**el profesor Cortez**
4. ciencias sociales	**la profesora Lenis**
5. almuerzo	
6. ciencias	**el profesor Gala**
7. educación física	**el profesor Fernández**
8. inglés	**la profesora Ochoa**

1. La clase de _____

2. La clase de _____

3. La clase de _____

4. La clase de _____

Actividad 3.1

There are not enough hours in the day to do everything we want to do. Listen to the following people being interviewed. What do they want more time for? In the blanks provided, write the number of the statement that corresponds to each picture.

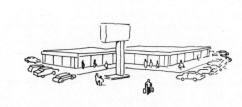

_____

_____

_____

_____

_____

_____

_____

_____

Actividad 3.2

What's in and what's out nowadays? Listen to the following activities and decide if they are "in" *(de moda)* or "out" *(pasado de moda)*. Put a check mark in the appropriate column. Then compare your opinions with the rest of the class.

DE MODA	PASADO DE MODA
1.	
2.	
3.	
4.	
5.	
6.	
7.	
8.	
9.	
10.	

Actividad 3.3

Four members of a crime ring have been hiding in your city. Listen as an agent from the Policía Internacional shows photos of the criminals to people on the street. Fill in the chart with the information the agent obtains.

INFORME POLICIAL

Nombre	Lugar	Día	Hora	Profesión
Lana La Roca				
Alfonso Crespo				
Pepita Jiménez				
Roberto Robles				

Actividad 3.4a

After listening to each of the following statements, decide if you think the excuses given are believable *(creíble)* or unbelievable *(increíble).* Be prepared to defend your answers with a partner after making your decisions.

EXCUSAS, EXCUSAS

Creíble	Increíble
1.	
2.	
3.	
4.	
5.	

Actividad 3.4b

Listen to the following couple trying to decide what they are going to do tonight. Every time an activity is mentioned that one of the two people wants to do, draw a circle around the picture. If the other person does NOT want to do that activity, draw an *X* through the picture. The pictures with circles only should represent what both people finally decide to do.

CAPÍTULO 4

Actividad 4.1

You are helping out a friend at the drive-through window of Restaurante La Calabaza in Mexico. Listen to the dialogues and record the quantity of each item ordered by each customer in the appropriate box of the chart.

RESTAURANTE LA CALABAZA

El almuerzo	Cliente 1	Cliente 2	Cliente 3	Cliente 4
Ensalada				
Hamburguesa				
Hamburguesa con queso				
Sandwich de pollo				
Sandwich de pescado				
Sandwich de jamón				
Sandwich de jamón y queso				
Papas fritas				
Papas al horno				

Actividad 4.2

While working at the Hotel María Cristina, you need to record breakfast orders for room service. Use the grid to make your report. First, listen carefully for the room number and write it in the appropriate box. Then write in the time requested. Finally, put a check mark next to each item ordered by the person in that room.

HOTEL MARÍA CRISTINA

	Habitación	Habitación	Habitación	Habitación	Habitación
Núm. de habitación					
Hora de servicio					
Jugo de naranja					
Jugo de tomate					
Cereal					
Pan tostado con mermelada					
Huevos fritos					
Jamón					
Café					
Té					
Leche					

Actividad 4.3

You are being asked to rate combination plates for a survey on upcoming menus in the school cafeteria. After you hear the description of each plate, mark your rating on the scale from 1 *(horrible)* to 5 *(muy sabroso)*.

	Horrible				*Muy sabroso*
1.	(1)	(2)	(3)	(4)	(5)
2.	(1)	(2)	(3)	(4)	(5)
3.	(1)	(2)	(3)	(4)	(5)
4.	(1)	(2)	(3)	(4)	(5)
5.	(1)	(2)	(3)	(4)	(5)
6.	(1)	(2)	(3)	(4)	(5)

Actividad 4.4a

You're at school waiting for assembly to start. You hear people behind you talking about your friends. Listen carefully so you can figure out whom they're talking about. Pay close attention to verb and adjective endings. Put a check mark in the appropriate column after each conversation.

	Daniel	Elisa	Daniel y sus amigos	Elisa y sus amigas
1.				
2.				
3.				
4.				
5.				
6.				

Actividad 4.4b

Two teachers and two students are on a discussion panel giving advice to teachers and students on how to get along better in school. Using the grid provided, listen and then check off the suggestions given by each of the panel members.

	Alicia (estudiante)	Sr. Rocas (profesor)	Raúl (estudiante)	Sra. Salinas (profesora)
Escuchar en clase				
Ayudar a otros estudiantes				
Ir a todas sus clases				
Comer un desayuno				
Leer en casa				
Estar en clase a tiempo				
Ser ordenados				
Ser trabajadores				
Ser pacientes				
Ser graciosos				

Actividad 5.1

Ana is showing Alejandro a picture of her family at a birthday party. Some of the people in the picture are family members, while others are family friends. Identify as many people as you can and write their names under their pictures. For those who don't belong to the family, write *amiga* or *amigo* in the blanks.

_____

_____

_____

_____

_____

_____

_____

Actividad 5.2

Listen and take notes as you overhear some friends talking about two people. Try to find out their name (*nombre*), age (*edad*), profession (*profesión*), and at least two physical characteristics (*características físicas*).

Primera Persona	Segunda Persona
Nombre:	**Nombre:**
Edad:	**Edad:**
Profesión:	**Profesión:**
Características físicas:	**Características físicas:**

Actividad 5.3

Five customers go to a department store to buy cologne for a person they know. Listen as each customer describes the person he or she has in mind to the salesperson. Write the name of each person described in the chart under the name of the cologne that best matches that person.

Colonia "Antídoto"

deportista

atrevido, -a

sociable

Persona: _____

Colonia "Bolero"

sensacional

cariñoso, -a

guapo, -a

Persona: _____

Colonia "Princesa"

práctico, -a

sofisticado, -a

elegante

Persona: _____

Colonia "Nueve a cinco"

serio, -a

conservador, -a

trabajador, -a

Persona: _____

Colonia "Compulsión"

sincero, -a

romántico, -a

callado, -a

Persona: _____

Actividad 5.4a

This semester's game show winners from the fourth- and fifth-period Spanish classes, Daniel and Jennifer, are competing for the championship. Correct answers earn them dollars toward a gift certificate to the school bookstore. As you hear the questions from each category, try to write down the answer in the blank before Daniel or Jennifer answers.

	FAMILIA	COMIDA	PASATIEMPOS	LA ESCUELA
$5	_____	_____	_____	_____
$10	_____	_____	_____	_____
$50	_____	_____	_____	_____
$100	_____	_____	_____	_____

Actividad 5.4b

Listen to the following people call in to Ana, their favorite talk-show host. All the callers have a problem with someone in their family. As you listen to each caller, take notes on their problems. After all the callers have spoken, write a sentence of advice for each caller. You may write your advice in English.

	PROBLEMA	CONSEJO
Maritza	_____	_____
	_____	_____
	_____	_____
Armando	_____	_____
	_____	_____
	_____	_____
Andrés	_____	_____
	_____	_____
	_____	_____
María Luisa	_____	_____
	_____	_____
	_____	_____

Actividad 6.1

What you wear can reveal secrets about your personality! Discover what type of message you send when you wear your favorite colors. As you listen to the descriptions, write down at least one word or phrase for each color in the grid. At the bottom of the grid, write in the blank what color you are wearing, and list one thing it says about you.

COLOR	PERSONALIDAD
Rojo	1.
Amarillo	2.
Morado	3.
Azul	4.
Anaranjado	5.
Marrón	6.
Gris	7.
Verde	8.
Negro	9.
Tu color:	Tu personalidad:

Actividad 6.2

Listen to the following items from one of the shopping services on TV. Even though you might not understand all the words (after all, it's a Spanish-language TV station), listen for words you know to help you identify the item. Then write down the price underneath the correct picture.

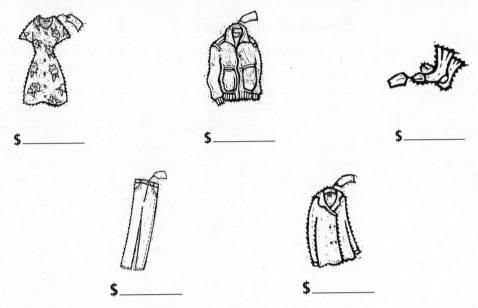

$_____ $_____ $_____

$_____ $_____

Actividad 6.3

Listen to the following people as they try to return unwanted items to the store. Write in the first column what type of clothing is described. Then check off in the appropriate box the reason for the return.

Tipo de ropa	Muy grande	Muy pequeño, -a	El color	No le gusta
1.				
2.				
3.				
4.				
5.				

Actividad 6.4a

Maritza is working at a laundry *(lavandería)* in Madrid. As the customers bring in their order, write the number of clothing items in each category in the appropriate boxes. Then total the amount of the order and write it in the blanks provided in the grid for each customer.

LAVANDERÍA LA PRINCESA

	Precios	Cliente 1	Ciente 2	Cliente 3	Cliente 4	Cliente 5
Blusas	$3.00					
Vestidos	$4.50					
Pantalones	$7.00					
Faldas	$4.00					
Suéteres	$3.50					
Camisas	$2.50					
Jeans	$6.00					
Chaquetas	$8.00					
Camisetas	$2.00					
	TOTAL					

Total para Cliente 1: $ _____

Total para Cliente 2: $ _____

Total para Cliente 3: $ _____

Total para Cliente 4: $ _____

Total para Cliente 5: $ _____

Actividad 6.4b

As you walk through "Galerías Españolas," you overhear several conversations between customers and salespeople. Match each conversation to one of the pictures provided. Write the number of the conversation under the corresponding picture.

_____   _____   _____   _____

CAPÍTULO 7

Actividad 7.1

See how well you know your geography facts of the world by listening to the following descriptions of places around the world. For each statement, put a check mark in the appropriate category in the chart.

LUGARES DEL MUNDO

	Las selvas tropicales	Las ciudades	Las pirámides	Los mares
1.				
2.				
3.				
4.				
5.				
6.				
7.				
8.				
9.				

Actividad 7.2

Listen to the following taped messages advising travelers on weather conditions in cities around the world during the month of December. For each message, enter the weather conditions for each city, as well as the high and low temperatures for the day.

	Condiciones del tiempo	Temp. máximas	Temp. mínimas
1. Moscú			
2. Lima			
3. Vancouver			
4. Ciudad de México			
5. Santiago			
6. Nueva York			

Actividad 7.3

Listen to the following descriptions and try to guess which month is being described. Write the name of the month on the appropriate line on the grid. Remember to listen for familiar words to help you guess correctly.

EL MES

1. _____

2. _____

3. _____

4. _____

5. _____

Actividad 7.4

To highlight National Math Week, each morning there is a problem to be solved during the morning announcements. While listening to the problem for each day of the week, take notes and see if you can write the correct answer at the end of the exercise. Friday's problem is super hard!

PROBLEMAS DE MATEMÁTICAS

1. ¿Cuántos juegan fútbol?   _____

2. ¿Cuántos piensan ir de vacaciones en agosto?   _____

3. ¿Cuántos no llevan ni impermeables ni paraguas?   _____

4. ¿Cuántos quieren visitar el museo?   _____

5. ¿Cuántos sandwiches de ensalada de huevo hay?   _____

Actividad 7.5

Some people travel long distances to practice their favorite sport. Listen to the departure dates of four people who boarded planes at different times of the year to practice the same sport.

For each date you hear, look at the grid below and find the name of the *month* given. Follow the column down to the *day* of the month given and circle the box where the two meet. The phrase in the box lists one item in the suitcase of the person traveling on that date. Once you have heard all four departure dates and circled the corresponding boxes, answer the question below the grid.

	ENERO	ABRIL	JULIO	OCTUBRE
2	los calcetines	el impermeable	los guantes	el abrigo
11	las botas	el cinturón	el bronceador	el sombrero
18	el gorro	la bufanda	los anteojos de sol	los guantes
25	el traje de baño	los tenis	los pantalones cortos	el gorro

¿Cuál es el deporte favorito de estos viajeros, esquiar en las montañas o bucear en el mar?

_____

Actividad 8.1

You always find something in the last place you look! Listen as people look for things they've misplaced somewhere in their house. After each conversation, complete the sentence that explains what each person is looking for and in which room it is found. Listen for clues in each conversation. (For example, the phrases *Busca* or *Está en*.)

1. El muchacho busca _____.

Está en _____.

2. La muchacha busca _____.

Está en _____.

3. La mujer busca _____.

Está en _____.

4. El niño busca _____.

Está en _____.

5. El hombre busca _____.

Está en _____.

Actividad 8.2

See if you can guess the prices of the items on the popular game show *¿Cuánto cuesta?* After listening to the descriptions of the furniture *(muebles)* and appliances *(aparatos)*, write down the name of the item and your estimated price while the clock is ticking. Check your prices with the real prices given by Don Gilberto at the end of the show.

¿CUÁNTO CUESTA?

	El mueble o aparato	El precio estimado	El precio correcto
1.			
2.			
3.			

Actividad 8.3

María Luisa and Pilar have very similar bedrooms. For each statement you hear, check off in the appropriate column whose bedroom is being described.

EL CUARTO DE MARÍA LUISA   **EL CUARTO DE PILAR**

	María Luisa	Pilar
1.		
2.		
3.		
4.		
5.		
6.		
7.		
8.		
9.		
10.		

Actividad 8.4

One of your summer jobs is to fill in the listings chart of available apartments. Listen to the following apartment advertisements and check off all the features mentioned in each ad.

	#252	#253	#254
Con muebles (amueblado)			
Un baño, un dormitorio			
Dos baños, dos dormitorios			
Dos baños, tres dormitorios			
Una cocina grande			
Un balcón			
Una vista espectacular			
Una piscina			
Cerca del centro comercial			
Acceso al gimnasio			
Aire acondicionado			
Mucha seguridad (security)			

Actividad 8.5

Your afternoon summer job is to find apartments for clients who call in to inquire. Listen to the following clients and match them with a specific apartment listing by referring to the chart used in *Actividad 8.4*.

1. Alicia Quintana   Apartamento # _____

2. Carmen Meléndez   Apartamento # _____

3. Enrique Bustón   Apartamento # _____

Actividad 9.1

Listen as the following people talk about activities that affect different parts of their body. After listening to each statement, determine which body part is being affected. Write the number of the statement underneath the corresponding item.

la espalda	**los dedos**	**la garganta**	**los ojos**	**el estómago**
_____	_____	_____	_____	_____

la nariz	**los brazos**	**la boca**	**los pies**	**las piernas**
_____	_____	_____	_____	_____

Actividad 9.2

Listen to the following statements. Decide whether the person is talking about a symptom *(síntoma)* or a remedy *(remedio)*, and put a check mark in the appropriate column.

	Síntoma	Remedio
1.		
2.		
3.		
4.		
5.		
6.		
7.		
8.		
9.		
10.		

Actividad 9.3

As part of your fitness plan, you need to know how many calories a 140-pound person can burn *(quemar)* performing various activities. Listen to each statement. On the grid, find the picture of the activity being described. Jot down the calories burned per 30 minutes, and place a check mark under each picture of the body part or parts on which the specific activity focuses.

	Calorías		

Actividad 9.4

As a volunteer for a local clinic, Lorena receives health information from people in the community. As she speaks with a woman who has called the clinic, help her fill in the woman's medical information on the blank card below. Follow the model.

Nombre: Luis Enrique Salas	**Síntoma:** dolor de oído
Edad: 45 años	**Médico:** Dr. Sullivan
Teléfono: 842-4877	**Hora / día:** 12 de enero / 4:00 de la tarde

Nombre:	**Síntoma:**
Edad:	**Médico:**
Teléfono:	**Hora / día:**

Actividad 9.5

Many people have waited in line all night to be the first to get tickets for a rock concert next month. Listen as a radio disc jockey interviews people in line. On the blanks below, write how long each person has been waiting.

Miguel _____ horas

Imelda _____ horas

Carlos _____ horas

Ana _____ horas

Paty _____ horas

Actividad 10.1

Listen while several of Rafael's friends tell him what they are going to do. See if you can predict where each person is going. Write the number of each conversation under the appropriate picture.

_____   _____   _____   _____

_____   _____   _____

_____   _____   _____

Actividad 10.2

Armando has been trying to catch up with his friend Mauricio all day. As he asks people where they have seen Mauricio last, write the time and place each person mentions in the blanks below. After you have heard all the people's answers, number the pictures in chronological order.

_____

_____

Actividad 10.3

The yearbook staff is identifying students' pictures for the yearbook. Look at the pictures from the senior class trip. Listen to the conversations and write the names of Javier, Marta, Marco, Graciela, Manuel, and Lupe under the correct pictures.

_____

_____

_____

_____

Actividad 10.4a

Listen as you hear several people describe a moment when they saw a stranger who they thought was attractive. After each statement, complete the sentences below with the correct location of the encounter.

1. Lo vio en _____

2. La vio en _____

3. Lo vio en _____

4. Lo vio en _____

5. La vio en _____

Actividad 10.4b

Listen to a radio announcer introduce baseball players on a baseball awards show for 1993. For each player, find the corresponding baseball card. Then complete the information on each card. You will write in the batting average *(promedio)*, number of years in the major leagues *(grandes ligas)*, and the home country of the player.

Nombre: José Rijo

Equipo: Rojos de Cincinnati

Promedio: _____

Años en las grandes ligas: _____

País de origen: _____

Nombre: Juan González

Equipo: Rangers de Texas

Promedio: _____

Años en las grandes ligas: _____

País de origen: _____

Nombre: Rafael Belliard

Equipo: Bravos de Atlanta

Promedio: _____

Años en las grandes ligas: _____

País de origen: _____

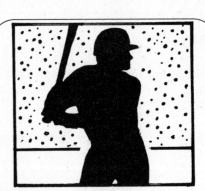

Nombre: Leo Gómez

Equipo: Orioles de Baltimore

Promedio: _____

Años en las grandes ligas: _____

País de origen: _____

Actividad 11.1

Listen to the television line-up for Channel 4. After listening to each program description, fill in on the grid the day or days the program is shown, the time it is shown, and the type of program it is.

LOS PROGRAMAS DEL CANAL 4

	Día(s)	Hora	Clase de programa
Mi computadora			
La detective Morales			
Cine en su sofá			
Las aventuras del Gato Félix			
Frente a frente			
Lo mejor del béisbol			
Marisol			
Festival			
Treinta minutos			
Las Américas			

Actividad 11.2

Listen to the following radio program in which listeners are asked trivia questions about the Guinness world records. After each question, write your answer on the lines. You can check your answers in *Actividad 11.3*.

Galerías de Guinness

1. _____

2. _____

3. _____

4. _____

5. _____

Actividad 11.3

See how well you answered the trivia questions from the previous activity. As you hear the announcer give the correct answer to each question, write it on the lines provided. Then compare your answers.

1. _____

2. _____

3. _____

4. _____

5. _____

CAPÍTULO 11

Actividad 11.4

Listen as you hear a film critic interview five people on opening night of the movie *Venecia*. After listening to each person, circle the number of stars that closely matches the person's opinion of the movie, from a low of one star to a high of four. After noting all the opinions, give the movie an overall rating of one to four stars, and give a reason for your answer.

	No le gustó nada	Le gustó más o menos	Le gustó mucho	Le encantó
1.	★	★★	★★★	★★★★
2.	★	★★	★★★	★★★★
3.	★	★★	★★★	★★★★
4.	★	★★	★★★	★★★★
5.	★	★★	★★★	★★★★

¿Cuántas estrellas *(stars)* para *Venecia*?

_____

_____

_____

_____

Actividad 11.5

Listen as the officers of the drama club discuss the people who auditioned for a part in the school play. After listening to each officer, check off in the grid each officer's choice for the part.

	Lupe	Gloria	Isabel	Verónica
Agustín				
Magda				
Fernando				
Olivia				

CAPÍTULO 12

Actividad 12.1

You and your friends have planned a party. Everyone is responsible for bringing something to eat or drink. Listen as two people go over the list to be sure everything is covered. Write the name of the person who is bringing each item on the line under the picture of the item.

Actividad 12.2

Listen as the following people call and complain to room service in the hotel. After each conversation, place a check mark in the column that describes the kind of complaint made.

Room number	Incorrect order	No silverware and/or condiments	Food is cold	Food not prepared correctly
233				
859				
692				
437				
528				

Actividad 12.3

Listen to the following conversations at a table in the Café La Rana Verde. After listening to what each person is saying, write the number in the corresponding dialogue bubble.

Actividad 12.4

Based on what you know about Mexican and Tex/Mex cuisine, see if you can guess which restaurant features certain dishes on their menu: the Café Hollywood in California, or the Café Miramar in Puerto Vallarta, Mexico. Put a check mark in the corresponding place on the grid.

	1	2	3	4	5	6	7	8
Café Hollywood								
Café Miramar								

Actividad 12.5

Listen as Gloria asks three of her friends what they did over the weekend. As you hear each response, put a check mark in the corresponding spot on the grid.

	Roberto sábado	Roberto domingo	Antonieta sábado	Antonieta domingo	Carlos sábado	Carlos domingo
Fue al gimnasio						
Visitó a sus abuelos						
Fue al cine						
Salió a mediodía						
Salió a las nueve						
Vio una entrevista						
Fue al museo con sus primos						
Comió en un restaurante						
Descansó						

Actividad 13.1

Listen to several students talk about the actions of other students with respect to the environment. If a student's action or actions had a positive impact on the environment, draw a happy face in the corresponding box or boxes. If a student's action or actions had a negative impact on the environment, draw a sad face in the corresponding box or boxes. At the end of the exercise, answer the question below the grid.

	José	Ana	Tony	Celi	Javier	Sonia
apagar la luz						
apagar la televisión						
montar en bicicleta						
llevar abrigo de piel						
reciclar						

En general, ¿los estudiantes sí están protegiendo el medio ambiente, o no?

Actividad 13.2

If animals could talk, how would they describe themselves? Listen to the following descriptions and identify the animal being described with a check mark.

	el oso	el lobo	el gorila	el tigre	el elefante	la ballena
1.						
2.						
3.						
4.						
5.						
6.						

Actividad 13.3

In honor of *El Día de la Tierra,* a local radio station is sponsoring a contest entitled *Nuestro Planeta, Nuestro Hogar.* As you listen to each statement, determine whether it is true *(verdadero)* or false *(falso)* and mark your answer on the grid below.

	1	2	3	4	5	6	7	8
Verdadero								
Falso								

Actividad 13.4

As you hear each of the following statements, imagine whom the speaker might be addressing. Choose from the list of people below, and write the number of the statement on the corresponding blank.

_____ al médico

_____ a la policía

_____ al camarero

_____ al empleado del hotel

_____ a sus amigos

_____ al empleado de la agencia de viajes

_____ a la profesora de español

_____ a sus padres

Actividad 13.5

Clarita is going to be visiting the Costa Rican rain forest this summer. Listen to various people giving her advice for her adventure. Put the number of the statement under the corresponding picture.

_____

_____

_____

_____

_____

_____

Actividad 14.1

Listen as friends ask for and offer advice on social situations. After each conversation, decide whether the advice is conservative *(conservador)* or daring *(atrevido),* and put a check mark in the appropriate box.

	1	2	3	4
Conservador				
Atrevido				

Actividad 14.2

Listen to the following message left on an answering machine. Circle the correct answer to each question from the three choices given.

¿Quién llamó?	Beti	Sara	Mónica
¿Cuál es la fecha de la fiesta?	15 de mayo	8 de mayo	11 de mayo
¿Y la hora?	6:00 de la tarde	3:00 de la tarde	7:00 de la tarde
¿Qué van a hacer en la fiesta?	nadar	bailar	ver la tele
¿Quién es uno de los invitados?	Tomás	Sergio	Nicolás
¿Dónde es la fiesta?	casa de Sara	casa de Mónica	casa de Beti
¿Qué tipo de fiesta es?	fiesta de fin de año	fiesta de sorpresa	fiesta de disfraces

Actividad 14.3

Listen to a girl describe a photo of a party to her sister, who was unable to attend. Write the name of each person described on the line that corresponds to each picture.

Actividad 14.4a

After listening to each of the following statements about school, decide if it is logical (*lógico*) or illogical (*ilógico*), and mark your answer on the grid. At the end of the exercise, compare your answers with those of a partner.

	1	2	3	4	5	6	7
Lógico							
Ilógico							

Actividad 14.4b

The teacher in charge of after-school detention is going to be absent for a few days. Listen as she describes the students to the substitute teacher. Write the name of each student in the blank under the corresponding picture.

_____

_____

_____

_____

_____

_____

_____

1 LA BAMBA

Para bailar la bamba, para bailar la bamba
se necesita una poca de gracia,
una poca de gracia y otra cosita
y arriba y arriba,
y arriba y arriba y arriba iré,
yo no soy marinero, yo no soy marinero,
por ti seré, por ti seré, por ti seré.

Bamba, bamba . . .

Una vez que te dije, una vez que te dije
que eras bonita, se te puso la cara,
se te puso la cara coloradita
y arriba y arriba,
y arriba y arriba y arriba iré,
yo no soy marinero, yo no soy marinero,
soy capitán, soy capitán, soy capitán.

Bamba, bamba . . .

Para subir al cielo, para subir al cielo
se necesita una escalera grande,
una escalera grande y otra chiquita
y arriba y arriba,
y arriba y arriba y arriba iré,
yo no soy marinero, yo no soy marinero,
por ti seré, por ti seré, por ti seré.

Bamba, bamba . . .

2 UNO DE ENERO

Uno de enero, dos de febrero,
tres de marzo, cuatro de abril,
cinco de mayo, seis de junio,
siete de julio, San Fermín.
(2X)

A Pamplona hemos de ir,
con una media, con una media.
A Pamplona hemos de ir,
con una media y un calcetín.

3 ERES TÚ

Como una promesa eres tú, eres tú
como una mañana de verano;
como una sonrisa eres tú, eres tú;
así, así eres tú.

Toda mi esperanza eres tú, eres tú,
como lluvia fresca en mis manos;
como fuerte brisa eres tú, eres tú
así, así eres tú.

(Estribillo):
Eres tú como el agua de mi fuente;
eres tú el fuego de mi hogar.
Eres tú como el fuego de mi hoguera;
eres tú el trigo de mi pan.
Algo así eres tú;
algo así como el fuego de mi hoguera.
Algo así eres tú;
mi vida, algo, algo así eres tú.

Como mi poema eres tú, eres tú;
como una guitarra en la noche.
Todo mi horizonte eres tú, eres tú;
así, así eres tú.

(Estribillo, 3X)

"Eres tú" by Juan Carlos Calderón. Reprinted by permission of
Hal Leonard Corporation.

4 HIMNO DEL ATHLETIC DE BILBAO

Tiene Bilbao un gran tesoro
que adora y mima con gran pasión.
Su club de fútbol
de bella historia,
lleno de gloria,
mil veces campeón.

Athletic, Athletic club
de limpia tradición,
ninguno más que tú
lleva mejor blasón.

Del fútbol eres rey,
te llaman el león
y la afición el rey
del fútbol español.

Cantemos pues los bilbainitos,
a nuestro club con gran amor,
para animarle con nuestro himno,
el canto digno del Alirón.

¡Alirón! ¡Alirón!
el Athletic es campeón.

5 LA MARIPOSA

Vamos todos a cantar,
vamos todos a bailar
la morenada.
(2X)

Con los tacos,
con las manos.
¡Viva la fiesta!
(2X)

6 PUERTO RICO

(Estribillo):
Puerto Rico, Puerto Rico
es mi tierra natal.
No la cambio por ninguna
aunque me paguen un capital.

(Estribillo)

Es la tierra de mis abuelos
de mi madre y de mi papá.
Puerto Rico, yo te adoro,
y no te puedo olvidar.

(Estribillo)

Ay, aunque me ofrezcan la luna
el cielo y el mar,
Puerto Rico, yo te adoro
y no te puedo olvidar.

(Estribillo)

Ay, mi madre siempre me dijo:
no te vayas a olvidar
que la tierra extraña;
acuérdate dónde está.

(Estribillo)

Ay, es la tierra de mis hermanos,
de mis abuelos y de mi mamá.
Puerto Rico, yo te adoro,
y no te puedo olvidar.

(Estribillo)

Ay, yo me encuentro en tierras extrañas;
yo te puedo cantar.
Puerto Rico, yo te adoro.
Tú eres de mi mamá.

(Estribillo)

Ay, aunque me ofrezcan la luna,
el cielo y el mar,
Puerto Rico, yo te adoro,
No te cambio por na'.

(Estribillo)

"Puerto Rico" by Marcial Reyes Arvelo from Puerto Rico, Puerto Rico, mi tierra natal. Produced by The Ethnic Folk Arts Center. Lyrics reprinted by permission of The Ethnic Folk Arts Center. Copyright (p) 1990 by Shanachie Entertainment Corporation. Used by permission of Shanachie Entertainment Corporation.

7 DE COLORES

De colores, de colores se visten los
    campos en la primavera.
De colores, de colores son los pajaritos
    que vienen de afuera.
De colores, de colores es el arco iris
    que vemos salir.
Y por eso los grandes amores de
    muchos colores me gustan a mí.
Y por eso los grandes amores de
    muchos colores me gustan a mí.

De colores, de colores brillantes y finos
    se viste la aurora.
De colores, de colores son los mil
    reflejos que el sol atesora.
De colores, de colores se viste el
    diamante que vemos lucir.
Y por eso los grandes amores de
    muchos colores me gustan a mí.
Y por eso los grandes amores de
    muchos colores me gustan a mí.

8 MARÍA ISABEL

La playa estaba desierta,
el mar bañaba tu piel,
cantando con mi guitarra
para ti, María Isabel.
(2X)

(Estribillo):
Toma tu sombrero y póntelo,
vamos a la playa, calienta el sol.
(2X)

Chiri biri bi, pompom pom pom pom.
(4X)

En la arena escribí tu nombre
y luego yo lo borré
para que nadie pisara
tu nombre: María Isabel.
(2X)

(Estribillo)

La luna fue caminando,
junto a las olas del mar;
tenía celos de tus ojos
y tu forma de mirar.

(Estribillo)
Chiri biri bi, pompom pom pom pom.

"María Isabel" by José Moreno Hurtado. Reprinted by permission of
EMI Music Publishing, Inc. and EMI Music Publishing, Spain.

9 CAMPO

(Estribillo):
Campo, yo vivo triste,
cada día sufriendo más.
¡Ay, Dios!, ¿qué será de mí?
Si no bailo esta bomba,
me voy a morir.

(Estribillo)

Oye, Campito, yo vivo triste,
cada día sufriendo más.
¡Ay, Dios!, ¿qué será de mí?
Si no bailo esta bomba,
me voy a morir.
¡Campo!

(Estribillo)

Sí, Mindonga, le digo a Maicolina,
Maicolina, échate pa' aquí.
¡Yo quiero bailar la bomba!
Si no la bailo, me voy a morir.
¡Campo, Campo!

(Estribillo)

Oye, Campito, yo vivo triste;
cada día yo sufro más.
¡Ay Dios!, ¿qué será de mí?
Si no bailo esta bomba,
me voy a morir.
¡Campo, Campo!

(Estribillo)

"Campo" from Puerto Rico, Puerto Rico, mi tierra natal. Produced by The Ethnic Folk Arts Center. Lyrics reprinted by permission of The Ethnic Folk Arts Center. Copyright (p) 1990 by Shanachie Entertainment Corporation. Used by permission of Shanachie Entertainment Corporation.

10 CANCIÓN CON TODOS

Salgo a caminar
por la cintura cósmica del Sur,
piso en la región
más vegetal del viento y de la luz;
siento al caminar
toda la piel de América en mi piel
y anda en mi sangre un río
que libera en mi voz su caudal.

Sol de Alto Perú,
rostro Bolivia, estaño y soledad;
un verde Brasil
besa a mi Chile cobre y mineral,
subo desde el sur
hacia la entraña América y total,
pura raíz de un grito
destinado a crecer y a estallar.

Todas las voces, todas;
todas las manos, todas;
toda la sangre puede
ser canción en el viento.
Canta conmigo, canta, latinoamericano,
libera tu esperanza
con un grito en la voz.
(2X)

"Canción con todos" by C. Isella and A. Tejada Gómez. Reprinted by permission of Sociedad Argentina de Autores y Compositores de Música (SADAIC), Argentina and Sociedad Argentina de Autores y Compositores de Música (SADAIC), Miami.

11 EN MI VIEJO SAN JUAN

En mi viejo San Juan
¡cuántos sueños forjé
en mis años de infancia!
Mi primera ilusión,
mis cuitas de amor
son recuerdos del alma.

Una tarde me fui hacia extraña nación,
pues lo quiso el destino.
Pero mi corazón se quedó frente al mar
en mi viejo San Juan.

(Estribillo):
Adiós (adiós, adiós)
Borinquen querida (tierra de mi amor)
Adiós (adiós, adiós)
mi diosa del mar (reina del palmar)
Me voy (ya me voy)
pero un día volveré
a buscar mi querer
a soñar otra vez
en mi viejo San Juan.

Pero el tiempo pasó;
el destino burló
mi terrible nostalgia.
Y no pude volver
al San Juan que yo amé,
pedacito de patria.

Mi cabello blanqueó, hoy mi vida se va;
ya la muerte me llama.
Y no quiero morir alejado de ti,
Puerto Rico del alma.

(Estribillo)

12 EL CONDOR PASA

Al cóndor de los Andes despertó
una luz,
una luz,
de un bello amanecer, amanecer.

Sus alas en lo alto extendió
y bajó,
y bajó,
al dulce manantial, para beber.

La nieve de las cumbres brilla ya
bajo el sol, el día y la luz.
La nieve de las cumbres brilla ya
bajo el sol, el día y la luz,
del bello amanecer, amanecer.

13 MÉXICO LINDO Y QUERIDO

Voz de la guitarra mía,
al despertar la mañana,
quiere cantar su alegría
a mi tierra mexicana.

Yo le canto a tus volcanes,
a tus praderas y flores
que son como talismanes
del amor de mis amores.

México lindo y querido
si muero lejos de ti
que digan que estoy dormido
y que me traigan aquí.

México lindo y querido
si muero lejos de ti
que digan que estoy dormido
y que me traigan aquí.

14 DÍAS DE AMAR

Vienen ya días de amar
La casa que habitas
Días de amar la tierra vegetal
Flor y animal
Vienen ya ríos con agua sin envenenar
Agua que beben los que tienen sed
Igual que usted
Vienen ya bosques pulmones de la gran ciudad
Selvas que aroman en la oscuridad Noches
    de paz
Que hacían falta a la humanidad

No es natural
Que en el planeta tanto ande mal
Que el hombre agreda al hombre
Que el hombre agreda al animal, al vegetal

Se oyen ya loras gritando a gran velocidad
Niños jugando con felicidad
Vuelvo a su edad
Pasan ya cosas que alegran a la humanidad
Aires que huelen como a Navidad en igualdad
Que hacían falta a la humanidad

No es natural
Que en el planeta tanto ande mal
Que el hombre agreda al hombre
Que el hombre agreda al animal, al vegetal

Vienen ya días de amar
El mundo que habitas
Días de amar la tierra vegetal
Flor y animal

15 LAS MAÑANITAS

Éstas son las mañanitas
que cantaba el Rey David,
pero no eran tan bonitas
como las cantan aquí.

(Estribillo, 2X):
Despierta, mi bien, despierta,
mira que ya amaneció,
ya los pajarillos cantan,
la luna ya se metió.

Si el sereno de la esquina
me quisiera hacer favor,
de apagar su linternita
mientras que pasa mi amor.

(Estribillo, 2X)

PRIMER PASO

Pronunciación. The letters *a* and *e*.

Spanish vowel sounds are not like English ones. First, each vowel usually has only one sound. Spanish vowel sounds are quicker and tenser than those in English, and they aren't drawn out.

a. The pronunciation of the letter *a* is similar to the vowel sound in the English word "pop."

The following words and phrases contain the letter *a*.

You will hear each word or phrase twice. After the first time, there will be a pause so you can pronounce it. Then you will hear the word or phrase a second time.

gracias

Ana María

Guatemala

España

adiós

Buenas tardes.

te llamas

b. The pronunciation of the letter *e* is similar to the sound of the *e* in the English word "get."

bien

Elena

mesa

estudiante

mes

enero

tres

CAPÍTULO 1

Pronunciación. The letter *i* and the word *y*.

The pronunciation of both the letter *i* and the word *y* is similar to the vowel sound in the English word "beet."

The following words and phrases contain the letter *i* or the word *y*.

You will hear each word or phrase twice. After the first time, there will be a pause so you can pronounce it. Then you will hear the word or phrase a second time.

y

sí

ir al cine

guitarra

A mí sí me gusta.

¿Y a ti?

impaciente

artístico, artística

CAPÍTULO 2

Pronunciación. The letter *o*.

The pronunciation of the letter *o* is similar to the vowel sound in the English word "coat."

The following words and phrases contain the vowel sound *o*.

You will hear each word or phrase twice. After the first time, there will be a pause so you can pronounce it. Then you will hear the word or phrase a second time.

o
yo
hora
español
No, lo siento.
¿Qué hora es?
Son las ocho.
Son las dos y cuarto.

CAPÍTULO 3

Pronunciación. The letter *u*.

The pronunciation of the letter *u* is similar to the vowel sound in the English word "boot."

The following words and phrases contain the vowel sound *u*.

You will hear each word or phrase twice. After the first time, there will be a pause so you can pronounce it. Then you will hear the word or phrase a second time.

tú
el lunes
estudias
ustedes
jugar fútbol
Me gustaría mucho.
un minuto
número uno

CAPÍTULO 4

Pronunciación. Rules for stressing syllables.

When you speak Spanish, you stress some syllables more than others, just as you do in English. There are a few simple rules that tell you which syllable of a Spanish word to stress.

a. When a word ends in a vowel or in *n* or *s,* the stress normally falls on the *next-to-last* syllable.

The following words are examples of this rule.

You will hear each word twice. After the first time, there will be a pause so you can pronounce it. Then you will hear the word a second time.

desayuno

tomate

ensalada

frutas

verduras

me encantan

b. When a word ends in any consonant other than *n* or *s,* the stress normally falls on the *last* syllable.

el cereal

el bistec

comer

beber

verdad

c. There are exceptions. In those cases an accent mark indicates where the stress falls.

jamón

plátano

café

también

suéter

CAPÍTULO 5

Pronunciación. The letters *ll* and *h.*

a. The pronunciation of the letter *ll* is similar to sound of the *y* in the English word "yard."

The following words and phrases contain the letter *ll.*

You will hear each word or phrase twice. After the first time, there will be a pause so you can pronounce it. Then you will hear the word or phrase a second time.

ellos

¿Cómo se llama?

Se llama Felipe del Castillo.

Ella es callada.

b. In Spanish, the letter *h* is never pronounced.

hermana

hijo

hombre

ahora

No hay gemelos en la clase.

CAPÍTULO 6

Pronunciación. The letters *r* and *rr.*

a. Except at the beginning of a word or after *l* or *n,* you pronounce the letter *r* by tapping the tip of your tongue once on the ridge behind your upper teeth. The sound is similar to the *dd* in the English word "ladder."

The following words and phrases contain the letter *r.*

You will hear each word or phrase twice. After the first time, there will be a pause so you can pronounce it. Then you will hear the word or phrase a second time.

barato, barata

caro, cara

negro, negra

zapatería

compré

para ti

otro, otra

por aquí

b. To make the sound of the letter *rr,* you tap your tongue several times on the ridge behind your front teeth.

guitarra

marrón

burrito

c. When *r* is the first letter of a word or comes after *l* or *n,* it is pronounced like the letter *rr.*

la ropa

rojo, roja

rubio, rubia

Rivera

Enrique

alrededor

CAPÍTULO 7

Pronunciación. The letters *b* and *v.*

a. In Spanish the letters *b* and *v* are pronounced alike. Except after a vowel, both are pronounced like the *b* in the English word "mob."

The following words and phrases contain either the letter *b* or the letter *v.*

You will hear each word twice. After the first time, there will be a pause so you can pronounce it. Then you will hear the word a second time.

bote

bucear

viento

¡Vaya!

vamos

b. When *b* and *v* come after a vowel, make the sound by bringing your lips together until they almost touch. This sound is softer than *b* or *v* in English.

subir

joven

Llueve.

Nieva.

sábado

llevar

CAPÍTULO 8

Pronunciación. The letters *d* and *t*.

a. Except after a vowel, the letter *d* is pronounced almost like the English *d*, but the tip of the tongue touches the inside of the upper teeth.

The following words and phrases contain the letter *d*.

You will hear each word or phrase twice. After the first time, there will be a pause so you can pronounce it. Then you will hear the word or phrase a second time.

dos

segundo

dormitorio

de metal

de cuero

b. After a vowel, *d* is pronounced almost like the "th" in the English word "mother."

una casa de dos pisos

comedor

césped

cuadro

equipo de sonido

moderno, moderna

c. When we pronounce the letter *t* in English, it is often followed by a little puff of air. In Spanish, the letter *t* is pronounced without this puff of air. The tongue is right behind the upper teeth.

cuarto

estar

platos

sótano

tener

escritorio

antiguo, antigua

CAPÍTULO 9

Pronunciación. The letters *p* and *ñ*.

a. The pronunciation of the letter *p* in English is often followed by a little puff of air. If you put your hand close to your mouth, you can feel the air when you say the word "popular." In Spanish, *p* is pronounced without this puff of air.

The following words contain the letter *p*.

You will hear each word or phrase twice. After the first time, there will be a pause so you can pronounce it. Then you will hear the word or phrase a second time.

pie

cuerpo

espalda

pierna

¿Qué pasa?

gripe

hospital

peor

b. The pronunciation of the letter *ñ* is similar to the sound of the *ny* in the English word "canyon."

tengo sueño

baño

cumpleaños

montaña

señor

señora

cariñoso, cariñosa

tacaño, tacaña

CAPÍTULO 10

Pronunciación. The letter combination *qu* and the letter *c*.

a. In Spanish the letter combination *qu* is pronounced like the letter c in the English word "cat." In English, that sound is usually followed by a puff of air. In Spanish it is not.

The following words and phrases contain the letter combination *qu*.

You will hear each word or phrase twice. After the first time, there will be a pause so you can pronounce it. Then you will hear the word or phrase a second time.

esquina

¿Qué quiere decir?

Queda a la izquierda.

quinientos

quitar la mesa

b. When the letter *c* comes before *a, o, u,* or a consonant, it is also pronounced like the *c* in "cat." Again, there is no puff of air.

banco

sacar

comunidad

comprar comestibles

a cuatro cuadras del correo

c. When *c* comes before *e* or *i*, most Spanish speakers pronounce it like the *s* in the English word "sand."

estación de policía

setecientos

hacer ejercicio

césped

cocina

vacaciones en la ciudad

a cinco cuadras

CAPÍTULO 11

Pronunciación. The letters *s, z,* and *ch*.

a. In Spanish, the letter *s* usually has the same sound as the *s* in the English word "sand."

The following words contain the letter *s*.

You will hear each word twice. After the first time, there will be a pause so you can pronounce it. Then you will hear the word a second time.

clase

sobre

demasiado

casi

hasta

b. The letter *z* in Spanish is usually pronounced like the *s*.

actriz

empieza

diez

plaza

almuerzo

izquierda

c. In Spanish, the letter *ch* has the same sound as the "ch" in the English word "check."

hechos

noche

muchacho

coche

leche

CAPÍTULO 12

Pronunciación. The letters *j* and *g*.

a. Pronunciation of the Spanish *j* is not like any English sound. It is a breathy sound, something like the *h* in the English word "hay," but it is made very far back in the mouth—almost in the throat.

The following words and phrases contain the letter *j*.

You will hear each word or phrase twice. After the first time, there will be a pause so you can pronounce it. Then you will hear the word or phrase a second time.

frijoles

junio

viaje

jueves

debajo

b. In a few words, the letter *x* has the same sound.

Texas

México

c. Before *e* and *i*, the letter *g* is pronounced just like the *j*.

generoso, generosa

gemelo, gemela

gimnasio

inteligente

d. After *n*, the letter *g* is pronounced like the *g* in the English word "get."

tengo

inglés

e. In all other cases, the *g* has a softer sound. The back of your tongue almost touches the roof of your mouth.

aguacate

traigo

abrigo

guacamole

f. In the groups *gue* and *gui,* the *u* is not pronounced.

guía

guitarra

en seguida

guisantes

CAPÍTULO 13

Pronunciación. The letters *i, u,* and *y* in diphthongs.

a. When the letter *i, u,* or *y* comes after a vowel, the two together form a combination called a diphthong. We pronounce diphthongs as one syllable.

The following words contain diphthongs.

You will hear each word twice. After the first time, there will be a pause so you can pronounce it. Then you will hear the word a second time.

hay

seis

aire

soy

ciudad

b. When the letter *i* or *u* comes after another vowel and has a written accent mark, the two vowels do not form a diphthong. We pronounce them as separate syllables.

país

Raúl

oído

c. When the letter *i* or *u* comes before another vowel, the two together form a diphthong and are pronounced as one syllable.

duele

aluminio

piel

jaguar

por supuesto

d. When the letter *i* or *u* comes before a vowel and has a written accent, the two vowels do not form a diphthong. We pronounce them as separate syllables.

energía

frío

día

dúo

CAPÍTULO 14

Pronunciación. The letter *l* and linking.

a. The letter *l* in Spanish has a similar sound to that of the *l* in the English word "leap." The tip of your tongue touches the ridge right behind your front teeth.

The following words and phrases contain the letter *l*.

You will hear each word or phrase twice. After the first time, there will be a pause so you can pronounce it. Then you will hear the word or phrase a second time.

escuela

baile

alguien

elegante

pulsera

el ambiente

mal

especial

b. You have probably noticed that when people speak Spanish, they often run words together without pausing in between. For example, the phrase *a la derecha de la casa* may sound more like two words than six. You don't think about it, of course, but we do the same thing in English. When you say "I'm going to go," it will probably sound like "I'm gonna go" or even "Ahmana go!" This combining of sounds is called linking. When the last sound of a word is the same as the first sound of the next word, we usually pronounce them as one sound.

el novio de Elena

los zapatos

va a bailar

c. We usually run two vowels together.

la escuela

para una amiga

hecha a mano

Te presento a Anita.

d. We often pronounce the final consonant as if it were the first letter of the next word.

el invitado

el ambiente

los animales

mal hecho, mal hecha

Video Activities

EL PRIMER PASO   Fecha _____

A ¡Piénsalo bien!

Welcome to the Spanish-speaking world! In the faces you saw in this segment, do you notice resemblances to persons you know or have seen? In the Spanish you hear, can you sense differences in the speed and clarity of speech, as with the English spoken by you and your friends?

B Vocabulario para conversar

1. Match the cities we will visit and our guides, then locate them on a map.

Guadalajara, México   Madrid, España   Miami, Florida

Guide	City
Alexander Ruiz	_____
Karina Romera	_____
Gracia Somolinos y Jorge Castillo	_____

2. Say "hello!" like Karina and Gracia! Then write it down.

_____

C Todo junto

1. In what order does Alexander meet these people at the Bayside Mall? Write "1" next to the name of the person he meets first, "2" next to the second person, and so on.

_____ Carlos Cruz   _____ Jorge

_____ Carolina   _____ Karina Johnson

_____ Corina Lopes   _____ Rubén Lopes

_____ Jessica   _____ Verónica

2. Do you recognize the names of some of the places where the people interviewed by Alexander come from? Tell a classmate two or three of the places. Do any of these surprise you? Think of one other city and country where speakers of Spanish are likely to be from.

_____

_____

A ¡Piénsalo bien!

1. Before watching this video segment: People everywhere enjoy a variety of leisure activities—playing music, practicing sports, and creating handicrafts, to name a few. Notice these kinds of pastimes as they are featured in the first video segment.

2. After watching this segment, fill in the grid below according to what you observed. Add other activities from the United States if you wish to, or activities that you yourself do personally.

Leisure-time Activities	Video illustration(s) from Hispanic Countries	Example(s) from the United States
a. music	_____	playing the piano
b. sports	_____	skiing, tennis
c. crafts	_____	beadwork, carving
d. other	_____	reading, watching TV

B Vocabulario para conversar

1. List some answers you would be likely to hear if you asked your friends, "What do you like to do in your spare time?" Then, after seeing the video segment, place a check mark next to all those activities mentioned by Alexander.

_____

_____

2. Say it like Alexander! After seeing the video segment a few times, repeat what Alexander has just said when your teacher pauses the tape. Examples:

¿Yo? ¿Cómo soy yo?

Soy deportista.

Me gusta practicar deportes.

Me gusta patinar.

Pero tengo que practicar más.

3. Use the words below to fill in the blanks and tell about Alexander's personality.

artístico　　callado　　deportista　　impaciente　　serio　　sociable

Soy _____ y _____.

A veces, soy _____: me gusta mucho leer.

No soy ni _____ ni _____.

No soy tampoco muy _____: no me gusta dibujar.

4. Tell what Alexander likes and dislikes doing by writing *sí* or *no* in the blanks below.

_____ Me gusta cocinar.

_____ Me gusta dibujar.

_____ Me gusta escuchar música.

_____ Me gusta estar con mis amigos.

_____ Me gusta tocar la guitarra.

C Todo junto

1. Watch this segment of the video carefully several times, then for each pair of possible answers, circle the one in each pair that received the most responses in Alexander's poll.

paciente	impaciente
trabajador(a)	perezoso(a)
deportista	no soy deportista
me gusta cocinar	no me gusta cocinar

2. How would you answer if Alexander asked you these questions?

ALEXANDER: ¿Cómo eres tú, paciente o impaciente?

YOU: _____

ALEXANDER: ¿Eres trabajador(a) o perezoso(a)?

YOU: _____

ALEXANDER: Soy deportista. ¿Y tú?

YOU: _____

ALEXANDER: A mí me gusta cocinar. ¿Y a ti?

YOU: _____

A ¡Piénsalo bien!

1. Before watching the video: All over the world, children and teenagers go to school every morning. What do you expect to see when first-graders leave the classroom for recess or a field trip? When high school students wait in the morning for school to start, or take a test, or listen to a lecture in class? Jot down one thing you might see in each situation.

2. After watching the video, compare your expectations with what you saw happening in these schools in Spanish-speaking countries. Did you observe any of the same things that you wrote down?

B Vocabulario para conversar

1. Let's spend the morning with Gracia at her high school in Madrid! Put a check mark next to all the things she has in her backpack, and circle the item she is looking for.

_____ una calculadora   _____ un libro

_____ una carpeta   _____ una mochila

_____ una carpeta de argollas _____ unos marcadores

_____ un cuaderno   _____ unas hojas de papel

_____ un lápiz   _____ una regla

2. What classes does Gracia have each period? Write down her schedule as you go through the day with her.

Primera hora   _____

Segunda hora   _____

Tercera hora   _____

Cuarta hora   _____

Quinta hora   _____

Sexta hora   _____

3. *Gracia y las artes.* . . . What opinions does Gracia share with us as she begins her homework? Circle what she tells us.

(Sé / No sé) dibujar muy bien.

(Soy / No soy) artística.

El arte es (difícil / fácil).

Me gusta más (el arte / la música).

C Todo junto

1. *Jorge habla con la profesora de español en una escuela de Madrid.* What do you notice about the Spanish classroom? How does it compare with your classrooms?

_____

_____

2. Ask two or three classmates some questions similar to the ones Jorge asks, and write down the answers you receive.

   a. ¿Cuántos(as) estudiantes hay en la clase de español?

   _____

   _____

   b. ¿Tienes mucha tarea? ¿En qué clase(s)?

   _____

   _____

   c. ¿A qué hora empieza tu clase favorita? ¿Qué necesitas para esa (*that*) clase?

   _____

   _____

3. Now that you have visited a school in Madrid with Gracia and Jorge, jot down one or two impressions you have of schools in Spain.

_____

_____

A ¡Piénsalo bien!

1. Before watching this video segment: People of all ages enjoy various leisure-time activities. What do you like to do when you have free time and the weather is warm? And when the weather keeps you indoors? Ask a classmate or two how they spend their free time. Do any of your favorite pastimes require group participation?

2. After watching the segment, list the leisure activities you saw taking place in the Spanish-speaking communities in this segment. Which require good weather? Which can be practiced alone?

B Vocabulario para conversar

1. Listen carefully as Gracia and Jorge welcome us! What exactly do they say?

JORGE: _____. _____ Jorge.

GRACIA: _____ Gracia.

2. *Dicen Jorge y Gracia, "Estamos en la Casa de Campo, el parque más grande y más antiguo de Madrid. Todos los días, puedes ver a muchas personas aquí haciendo muchas cosas . . ."*
Circle the activities that we see happen in the park.

Hay personas que . . .

van de compras   van al cine

van de pesca   van al zoológico

van en bicicleta   juegan básquetbol

van a la piscina   juegan béisbol

van a la playa   juegan tenis

3. *¡Vamos al parque de diversiones! ¿Cómo está Jorge?*

un poco cansado   un poco enfermo   un poco ocupado

CAPÍTULO 3

Fecha _____

C Todo junto

1. According to Jorge and Gracia. . . . *¿Cuál es el pasatiempo más popular en España?*

_____

2. Here are some phrases you will hear Gracia and Jorge say. Can you figure out what they mean, from context and related English words?

el fútbol

JORGE: . . . los componentes del club de Oroquieta, que son las campeonas de Europa de fútbol femenino.

_____

_____

GRACIA: Ella es la jugadora más joven en el equipo.

_____

las fiestas de la región

las corridas de toros: _____

3. *¿Te gusta bailar?* How many people would you estimate are enjoying the street dance? What do you think the ages might be of the youngest and oldest dancers you see?

_____

_____

4. Imagine that Jorge and Gracia invite you to attend these three events with them! Respond to their invitations.

¿Quieres jugar fútbol con nosotros?

_____

¿Quieres ir a la corrida de toros?

_____

¿Quieres bailar?

_____

A ¡Piénsalo bien!

1. Every day people all over the world enjoy meals at home or in restaurants, shopping for special foods, and preparing favorite dishes.

After you have seen the video, be prepared to comment about something you especially noticed regarding one of the activities.

eating a meal   preparing food   purchasing food

2. Tell a classmate about the scene you especially noticed. In which of these settings might it have been filmed? What makes you think this?

in the home of a Hispanic family in the U.S.   in a Mexican town

B Vocabulario para conversar

1. Circle the appropriate word or phrase to describe Gracia and Jorge's excursion at the marketplace.

Gracia y Jorge están en el mercado de San Miguel (en Barcelona / en Madrid).

Son las ocho (de la mañana / de la noche).

Gracia quiere (un té / un café), pero no lo sirven en el mercado.

Aquí venden de todo: todo tipo de (frutas, verduras y carnes / cuadernos, libros y mochilas).

Despues, Gracia tiene (hambre / sed) y quiere (comer algo / beber algo).

Ella (come patatas fritas / bebe un zumo de naranja).

Jorge dice (¡Qué asco! / ¡Qué sabroso!).

Jorge va a comprar los ingredientes (para una cena buena para la salud / para un almuerzo sabroso).

2. Observe Jorge's hand gestures (a) when he says *Bueno, más o menos* and (b) when he indicates *No, gracias*. Practice these gestures with a partner.

3. Here are some of the items pictured at one of the stands in the marketplace. Can you add other things to the list that might be sold at the same stand?

cebollas   endibias   lechuga   naranjas   plátanos

c Todo junto

1. Respond to suggestions from Jorge and Gracia as you shop together for ingredients to prepare lunch.

GRACIA: ¿Qué prefieres beber? A mí me gustan los refrescos.

YOU: _____

GRACIA: Debemos comer algo. ¿Te gustan las patatas fritas?

YOU: _____

JORGE: Bueno, vamos a comprar los ingredients para el almuerzo. ¿Qué tipo de carne prefieres?

YOU: Me encanta(n) _____

JORGE: ¿Y qué verduras te gustan?

YOU: A mí me gustan _____

JORGE: Bueno, ¡vamos a comprar todo lo que necesitamos!

2. Gracia and Jorge went to several different shops or stands to purchase the ingredients for their meal. See if you can remember three different places and what they purchased at each. Write the names of the places and the foods in Spanish.

a. _____

b. _____

c. _____

3. In cities in Spain and Latin America, people often can choose between shopping for food at a modern supermarket or at a traditional marketplace, as Jorge and Gracia did. After viewing the video, can you state an advantage offered by each?

Marketplace _____

Supermarket _____

CAPÍTULO 5

A ¡Piénsalo bien!

1. Before watching this video segment: As in most cultures, Hispanic families enjoy spending time together—grandparents, parents and children; uncles, aunts, and cousins. With a classmate, list several leisure activities that families can enjoy together, both in the home and outside.

2. After watching this segment, compare your list of family activities with those you saw in the segment. Are any of them the same? What are families in the United States likely to do together?

B Vocabulario para conversar

1. Karina describes several of her family members to us. Circle all the words you hear her use to talk about the following people.

   a. su papá

   alto   44 años   guapo   pelo castaño   simpático

   b. su mamá

   39 años   guapa   inteligente   ojos azules   sociable

   c. su hermano

   14 años   cariñoso   gemelo   menor   mayor   ojos negros

2. *¿De quién son estos apellidos?* Match the people or pets with the correct last names.

   a. Romera Herrera   **i.** la gata y la perra de Karina

   b. Romera Scott   **ii.** la mamá de Karina

   c. Scott de Romera   **iii.** el papá de Karina

C Todo junto

1. *Todos los domingos, la familia de Guadalupe Carrillo vienen a comer.* Can you pick out the names of the oldest and the youngest of the eight Carrillo brothers and sisters?

   Los hijos Carrillo: Gabriel, Javier, Jorge, Pepe, René

   _____ es el hijo mayor, hermano de Guadalupe.

   _____ , _____ y _____ son los otros hermanos;

   _____ es el hijo más joven.

   Las hijas Carrillo: Angélica, Guadalupe, Marta

   _____ es la hija mayor.

   _____ es la hija menor.

2. Karina interviews Jorge's family. See if you can write down some of the things mentioned or that you noted about the children.

	JORGE	BIANCA
¿Cuántos años tiene?	_____	_____
¿De qué color tiene el pelo?	_____	_____
¿Quién es el mayor y quién es el menor?	_____	_____
¿Cómo es?	_____	_____
	_____	_____
	_____	_____

3. About how many people seem to be at the Carrillo family dinner? What were some of the relationships among the people present? With a classmate, discuss how a weekly gathering like this might effect the way people think about "family."

_____

_____

4. Most of us have probably seen a family photo album like Karina's, but maybe we have never experienced a "family photo history room" like Guadalupe Carrillo's. What does this suggest to you about the role of her family in Guadalupe's life?

_____

_____

A ¡Piénsalo bien!

1. Before watching this video segment: Are you a person who enjoys shopping? When you want to buy a new clothing item, do you have a favorite store, or do you enjoy looking around? What different possibilities for purchasing clothes are there in your community? Discuss with a classmate different kinds of places you know that offer various price ranges and clothing specialties.

2. After watching this segment, did you see any merchandise outlets that looked expensive? Inexpensive? Any that seemed to specialize in a particular kind of merchandise? Discuss your impressions with a classmate, and state which shops you would like to visit if you had the chance.

B Vocabulario para conversar

1. Jorge tells us the name of the monument where he and Gracia meet. What does he say?

   a. Ésta es la estatua de Cristóbal Colón.

   b. Ésta es la estatua de Don Quixote.

   c. Ésta es la estatua de El Greco, el artista.

2. *¡Jorge y Gracia no están de acuerdo!* Indicate which person made these statements about shopping at El Rastro.

   El mejor lugar para ir de compras es El Rastro. La ropa es mucho más barata.

   _____

   Allí es horrible. Siempre hay muchísimas personas.

   _____

3. Jorge and Gracia talk about lots of clothing!

   a. What is another word for "jeans" used in Spain? _____

   b. What merchandise does Gracia mention on her way to Cortefiel?

   _____

   c. What merchandise does she show us in the store itself? See how many things you can remember and write down.

   _____

4. When can we shop at El Rastro, according to Jorge? What can we buy there?

_____

C Todo junto

1. Jorge hears many vendors shouting out as he walks through El Rastro. What kinds of things are people likely to be calling out about?

_____

2. Write down some of the answers to the questions Gracia and the saleslady ask each other. Then, with a classmate, create your own dialogue using the same questions, but changing the responses.

¿Qué deseas? _____

¿Son para ti? _____

¿Qué color quieres? _____

¿Qué estilos tiene? _____

_____

¿Quieres probártelos? _____

¿Cómo te quedan? _____

¿Cuánto cuestan? _____

¿Te los vas a llevar puestos? _____

¿Vas a pagar en efectivo o con tarjeta de crédito? _____

3. After visiting both El Rastro and Cortefiel, write down one or two advantages of shopping at each. Which do you prefer and why?

_____

A ¡Piénsalo bien!

1. Before watching this video segment: If you could spend your next vacation doing anything you wanted to, what would you do? Travel? Relax at home? Visit a local place of interest? Notice how these choices are reflected in this segment featuring places to go on vacation.

2. After watching this segment, which of the vacation activities you saw was most appealing to you? Think about where it might have been filmed, based on what you know about the geography and attractions of Spanish-speaking cities and nations.

B Vocabulario para conversar

1. Find Guadalajara on the map of Mexico, on p. XIV of your textbook. What do you think the weather is like there?

2. Karina shows us her favorite things to do in Guadalajara. Match each of the places with something interesting she tells us.

Este lugar...	**es interesante porque...**
_____ la Catedral	**a.** es un lugar donde se puede escuchar a los mariachis.
_____ la Plaza de las Américas	**b.** es el lugar más conocido de Guadalajara.
_____ el Palacio de Gobierno	**c.** hay murales de José Clemente Orozco y nos dicen la historia de la gente de México.
_____ la Cola de Caballo	**d.** hay rodeos mexicanos todos los domingos.
_____ el Lienzo Charro, Ignacio Cermeño	**e.** hay unas cataratas pequeñas.

3. Karina has told us what she likes to do in Guadalajara. Based on what you have seen, where would you choose to go to do each of the following?

Me gustaría ir a _____ para sacar fotos de

ese lugar, porque _____.

Quiero visitar _____ como lugar de

interés, porque _____.

Para descansar, prefiero ir a un lugar como _____ porque

_____.

4. If you were to visit the center of Guadalajara, what would you see, according to the video segment?

_____

C Todo junto

1. The people of Guadalajara love their city! Watch this segment of the video several times, then write down an answer or two that Karina hears when she asks for advice to give to tourists visiting Guadalajara. Compare your responses with a classmate.

a. Si un amigo viene a visitarte, ¿adónde lo llevarías tú?

_____

b. ¿Qué crees que la gente se puede llevar como recuerdo de aquí, de Guadalajara?

_____

c. ¿Qué le recomiendas que traiga en la maleta?

_____

d. ¿Qué crees que tenga de especial Guadalajara?

_____

2. Now that you have toured Guadalajara with Karina, write a paragraph or two about it for your travel diary. You might mention your first impressions of Karina, of the city, and your plans for tomorrow. When you finish, share your work with a classmate or keep it in your portfolio.

Here are some expressions that you may want to use.

Estoy en Guadalajara con Karina. Ella . . .

Guadalajara es una ciudad muy . . .

Hay mucho que hacer aquí; por ejemplo . . .

Mañana vamos a . . .

Estoy muy . . . porque . . .

A ¡Piénsalo bien!

1. Before watching this video segment: Imagine that a Spanish friend asked you to describe a "typical American house" where you live. How would you answer? List your ideas, then discuss them with a classmate. Consider how climate and other conditions might influence what is "typical."

2. After viewing the film segment showing Spanish homes and architecture, collaborate with your classmate to develop a list of architectural features that you might name if you were asked to describe a "typical" Spanish house.

B Vocabulario para conversar

1. Jorge and Gracia will take us to visit El Escorial! *Pero ellos tienen que hacer algunos quehaceres en casa antes de salir.* See if you can identify who has which task to do.

_____ Arreglo mi cuarto y hago mi cama.

_____ Tengo que lavar la ropa.

_____ Mi hermana me dice que tengo que lavar los platos antes de irme.

_____ Estoy sacudiendo los muebles.

_____ Tengo que pasar la aspiradora.

_____ Tengo que poner la mesa.

_____ Tengo que sacar la basura.

2. *¿Quieres ayudarme?* With a classmate, pretend you are Gracia or Jorge, and invite your classmate to help with the chores mentioned above. He or she will accept or offer a polite excuse. For example, you might say, *"Tengo que arreglar mi cuarto y hacer mi cama. ¿Quieres ayudarme?"*

_____

_____

3. Of the rooms you saw in Jorge's and Gracia's homes, which resembled rooms in houses you are familiar with? Which seemed different, and how were they different?

_____

_____

Capítulo 8

C Todo junto

1. *¡Qué bello es el palacio de El Escorial!* Circle some of the words that Donato del Prado, *nuestro guía,* uses to describe it.

está lejos de Madrid

hay 850 cuartos

es un monasterio

construido en el siglo dieciséis

es un monumento importante

hay nueve torres

hay muchos balcones

hay unas cocinas modernas

2. Listen carefully and then circle the correct dates! *Dice el señor Prado:*

"Se empezaron los trabajos en (1442 / 1563) y se terminaron en (1463 / 1584) —veintiún años."

3. Imagine a friend of yours is going to visit El Escorial. What would you tell him or her to notice during the visit?

En la basílica vas a ver: _____

y en la biblioteca hay . . . _____

y en el dormitorio del rey Felipe puedes ver . . . _____

y hay otras cosas también: _____

4. How would you answer Gracia's question to Jorge: *¿Te gustaría vivir aquí?*

_____

_____

A ¡Piénsalo bien!

1. Before watching this video segment: Most people are fortunate to be able to take good health for granted . . . but have you ever thought about what it would be like to be hospitalized for an illness or injury? Or perhaps you or someone you know has already spent time in a hospital. What are some things that might make a hospital stay comfortable and reassuring for a patient? Jot down some ideas, then share your thoughts with a classmate.

2. After watching this segment, did you notice if any of the things you mentioned above were depicted in the hospital scenes? What instances did you observe of family members dealing with health problems together, or participating in healthful activities together?

B Vocabulario para conversar

1. *¡Pobre Gracia! ¿Qué dice ella?*

"Me siento muy mal. Me duele todo.

Creo que tengo _____.

Tengo dolor de _____."

2. Jorge has some questions and suggestions for Gracia. *¿Qué dice él?*

"Comiste demasiada _____.

Vamos a ir a un _____.

Debes comer bien y hacer _____.

. . . el ejercicio es bueno para el _____.

¿Tienes frío? Aquí tienes mi _____."

3. Imagine you overhear Gracia describing her symptoms to the doctor. Write *sí* or *no* to the sentences below as she tells him what hurts.

_____ Me duele la boca.

_____ Me duele el estómago.

_____ Me duele la garganta.

_____ Me duelen los oídos.

_____ Me duelen los ojos.

_____ Tengo fiebre.

Nombre _____

Fecha _____

1. Let's go with Jorge and Gracia to their flamenco dancing class! Watch the first part of this video segment several times, then identify what you notice as special features of this kind of dancing. Compare your observations with a classmate and discuss special features of traditional American dances you might know about, such as square dancing.

_____

_____

2. Listen carefully as Lucía Real and El Camborio answer our hosts' questions. Jot down a few of their responses.

   GRACIA: ¿Qué parte del cuerpo se usa más para bailar?

   _____

   JORGE: Yo creo que la espalda es muy importante para estos bailes, ¿no?

   _____

3. After the dance lesson, how do Gracia and Jorge feel?

   GRACIA: _____

   JORGE: _____

   _____

4. Imagine that you had the opportunity to interview Lucía Real and El Camborio about their flamenco dancing. What question would you ask them?

   _____

CAPÍTULO 10

A ¡Piénsalo bien!

1. Whether we live in a big city, a small town or in the country, most of us leave our homes every day and go into our communities in order to work, go to school, take care of business, or enjoy ourselves.

Of the places featured in the Hispanic communities shown in this video segment, name one or two that are usually found in large cities. Name one or two that may be found in any community. Which of these do you have in your own community?

2. What different modes of transportation are used by people in this video segment? Which ones did you use yesterday?

B Vocabulario para conversar

1. Can you remember the order of the places Alexander visited in this segment? Write "1" next to the place he went first, "2" next to his second destination, and so on. Then circle the reason that he went to each place.

Compare your responses with those of a classmate, then watch the video segment again to verify your responses.

ALEXANDER: "Esta mañana . . .

_____ fui al correo y le envié un regalo (a mi amigo en Orlando / a mi tía en Cuba).

_____ fui al banco y (saqué dinero / deposité dinero).

_____ fui a la farmacia y compré (unas pastillas para la garganta y una tarjeta de

cumpleaños / un bolígrafo y unas hojas de papel).

_____ fui al mercado y compré (unos vestidos / algunos comestibles).

_____ fui a la tienda de regalos. Allí le compré (una gorra a mi amigo /

un libro a mi tía)."

2. Fill in the blanks with the mode of transportation Alexander used to get to where he was going that morning. Select your answer from the following choices:

a pie   en autobús   en coche   en taxi

ALEXANDER: "Yo fui _____ al correo.

Fui _____ a la farmacia.

Fui _____ a la tienda de regalos."

C ¡Todo junto!

1. ¿Quién lo hizo? Match the person with the answer he or she gave to Alexander's question, *"¿Adónde fuiste tú esta mañana?"*

_____ la joven

_____ cliente del barbero

_____ el barbero

a. Yo estaba dormido.

b. Yo fui a la farmacia y compré sellos.

c. Yo fui al colegio.

2. ¿Por qué fueron al banco? Repeat the answers Alexander receives when he asks, *"¿Qué hizo usted hoy en el banco?"*

3. ¿Dónde está la librería? Complete the description of the bookstore's location by filling in the blanks with the words you hear Alexander say.

ALEX: "Por fin llegué. La librería está en la _____ ocho, entre la

avenida _____ y la avenida _____."

4. ¡Ahora te toca a ti! Ask a classmate two of Alexander's survey questions, then answer two different ones that he or she will ask you.

¿Adónde fuiste tú esta mañana?

¿Dónde queda la estación de bomberos?

¿Qué hizo Ud. hoy en el banco?

¿Te gusta más el metro o el autobús? ¿Por qué?

¿Dónde está la librería?

A ¡Piénsalo bien!

1. In every corner of the world, people of all ages spend time daily relaxing in front of the television. Place a check mark next to the kinds of programs you see represented in these clips from Spanish-languge television shows.

_____	cartoon	_____	news program
_____	comedy program	_____	soap opera
_____	interview / social documentary	_____	sports program
_____	musical show	_____	talk show
_____	nature documentary	_____	weather forecast

2. If you were choosing a show to watch, which of the ones you saw would you select? Why?

B Vocabulario para conversar

1. At the beginning, what time does Alexander say it is? _____

2. Alexander states his preferences about films. Listen to what he says several times, then fill in the missing words to accurately reflect his feelings about movies.

ALEXANDER: ¿Te interesa ver una película?

Es una película de _____.

Esa clase de película es _____.

¡Pero me dan _____!

Ésta es muy _____.

Es una película de aventuras.

Las películas de aventuras me gustan mucho _____ que las

películas _____.

Las películas románticas son muy _____.

Me gustan _____ que las películas de _____.

3. Listen closely! Alexander states advantages offered by both television and movies, but which of the two does he prefer?

_____ El cine porque hay menos anuncios.

_____ La televisión porque tiene más variedad.

C Todo junto

1. What time does Alexander say it is now? _____

2. Alexander receives many different responses when he surveys people at the CocoWalk Mall about their movie preferences. Watch this video segment several times, then see if you can write down one or two answers people give to Alexander's questions, and their reasons for their responses.

ALEXANDER: ¿Quién es el mejor actor de cine?

RESPONSE(S): _____

ALEXANDER: Las películas de terror me dan miedo. ¿Y a ti?

RESPONSE(S): _____

ALEXANDER: ¿Te interesa ver una película de aventuras?

RESPONSE(S): _____

ALEXANDER: ¿Te interesa ver una película de ciencia ficción?

RESPONSE(S): _____

ALEXANDER: Me gusta más el cine. . . . (¿Y a ti?)

RESPONSE(S): _____

3. Ask some classmates one of Alexander's survey questions. Be sure to ask them *"¿Por qué?"* to learn the reasons for their answers.

_____

_____

_____

A ¡Piénsalo bien!

1. Before watching this video segment: When we go out to a restaurant, we often choose different kinds of food establishments for different kinds of occasions. Think about where teenagers like to go in your community, or where families go for dinner or to celebrate special occasions. How do these places differ in the food that is served? In price range? In atmosphere?

As you will see in the first video segment, just like in the United States, there are many different kinds of restaurants in Spanish-speaking countries.

2. After watching the segment, which of the eating establishments you saw looked like a nice place to spend the afternoon with a friend? Which one would be appropriate for a special, impressive dinner? Which one looked as if it might have a large university-student clientele? What did you notice about each that led you to your conclusions?

B Vocabulario para conversar

1. Before you watch this segment, think about your favorite restaurant. What makes it special?

2. After visiting Karina's favorite restaurant, what do you think she might say to explain why she likes it so much?

Es un restaurante _____.

Hay _____.

Los camareros son _____.

La comida es _____.

3. Karina talks about lots of delicious dishes! Put a check mark next to the names of those that she actually ordered, that day and the day before.

Platos principales	Bebidas	Otras comidas
_____ burritos	_____ agua	_____ chiles
_____ chilaquiles	_____ café	_____ frijoles refritos
_____ chiles rellenos	_____ jugo	_____ guacamole (aguacate)
_____ enchiladas	_____ leche	_____ postres
_____ quesadillas	_____ refrescos	_____ salsas
_____ tacos	_____ té	_____ tortillas de maíz/harina

CAPÍTULO 12

Fecha

C Todo junto

1. *Araceli Arrollo, la cocinera de La Paloma, está preparando unos platos. ¿Con qué se hacen estos platos?* Match each dish with the appropriate ingredients.

_____ burritos   **a.** tortillas de maíz, pollo, queso, chile verde o rojo, crema y lechuga

_____ enchiladas   **b.** tortillas de harina, frijoles, carne, salsa, crema y lechuga

2. Karina asks, *"¿Qué tipo de postre tienen aquí en La Paloma?"* Name one thing you heard or saw.

_____

3. Read below several questions that Karina asks, and the answers she receives. Then watch this segment of the video several times, listening carefully, until you can match the questions and answers with the appropriate interview situation.

a. **PREGUNTA:**   De los platos principales del menú, ¿cuál es lo que más les gusta?
    RESPUESTA: A mí, los que más me gustan son los burritos.
    PREGUNTA: ¿Están picantes tus burritos?
    RESPUESTA: No, no están picantes.

b. **PREGUNTA:**   ¿A ti?
    RESPUESTA: A mí me gustan mucho las papas.
    PREGUNTA: ¿Y a ti?
    RESPUESTA: También los chilaquiles, es una de las cosas que más me gustan, junto con las enchiladas.

c. **PREGUNTA:**   ¿Qué es lo que tú estás comiendo ahora?
    RESPUESTA: Un taquito de frijolitos, un taquito de carnita de pollo y un taquito de guacamole.

d. **PREGUNTA:**   ¿Te gusta el picante?
    RESPUESTA: Sí, a mí me gusta el picante.

_____ los tres jóvenes

_____ los dos jóvenes, el muchacho y la muchacha

_____ la madre y su hija

_____ la mujer

A ¡Piénsalo bien!

1. Before watching this video segment: It seems that everywhere, the earth's environment is endangered, and people are seeking solutions to help. What are some environmental issues that you are aware of concerning the sea? The mountains and forests? Large and small cities? Your own region? With a classmate, discuss and list some environmental concerns.

2. After watching this segment, add to your list any additional issues you saw depicted. Think of the ways you saw people working on environmental problems. Can you think of some things to do to address some of the concerns on your list?

B Vocabulario para conversar

1. After visiting the recycling center with Karina in Guadalajara, jot down some of the things that are separated and recycled there.

_____

_____

2. *Dice Karina, "Todas las mañanas, trabajadores recogen la basura para reciclarla."* What do people put in the different colored recepticles?

   El blanco es el del _____.

   El gris es el del _____.

   El amarillo es el del _____.

   El azul es el del _____.

3. How else could Karina say these things? Express the same idea by replacing the underlined phrases with words from the list below.

   conservar   recicla   recipientes

   KARINA: "Monto en bicicleta porque es una manera fácil de <u>ahorrar</u> energía."

   KARINA: "Aquí se <u>hace reciclaje de</u> papel de la ciudad."

   KARINA: "Éstos son los <u>cubos</u> especiales para reciclar."

C Todo junto

1. *¡Visitemos el zoológico con Karina!*

a. Watch this segment of the video several times, then see how many names you can write of animals that you saw at the Guadalajara zoo.

_____

_____

b. What else did you see besides animals?

_____

_____

2. By what title does Karina address the zoo guide? What does this show?

_____

3. Karina and the zoo guide discuss many different topics. In what order do they talk about the following things?

_____ El ambiente natural de los animales.

_____ Lo que se puede hacer para reducir la contaminación.

_____ Lo que pueden hacer las personas para cuidar a los animales y el medio ambiente.

_____ Los animales (especies) en peligro de extinción.

4. Imagine that you are responsible for greeting visitors to the Guadalajara zoo and conducting the first part of the tour, which Karina will then continue.

Develop a talk to guide visitors through the parts of the zoo depicted in the first part of this segment, before we meet Karina, telling briefly about the things we see. Below are some words and phrases which may be useful.

¡Bienvenidos!

Aquí estamos . . .

El tigre . . . el mandril . . . la jirafa

A ¡Piénsalo bien!

1. Before watching this video segment: Many communities in the United States, large and small, have special celebrations during the year: for example, winter or summer festivals; historical commemorations; religious or cultural events. Think of a community celebration that you know about, or that you are part of. What are some of the activities that make it special?

2. After watching this segment several times, share your impressions with a classmate. What did you observe in these celebrations that made them special? What was happening?

B Vocabulario para conversar

1. Listen carefully!

a. What are Karina's first words to us in this segment?

¡Buenos días!　　¡Buen provecho!　　¡Qué bueno!　　¡Qué suerte!

b. Why does she say this?
Porque nos han invitado a una fiesta muy especial en casa de la familia Blas Méndez.
Es una fiesta:

de fin de año　　de cumpleaños　　de los quince años　　de disfraces
　　　　　　　de los padres　　de las hermanas gemelas

2. ¿Qué regalo compra Karina para la fiesta?

_____

3. Write the letter of the statement that explains why Karina decides not to wear each of these things.

_____ su traje de baño　　　　**a.** No es una fiesta de gala.

_____ su traje de payaso　　　**b.** No es una fiesta de la playa.

_____ su vestido rojo　　　　　**c.** No le gusta llevarlos.

_____ sus zapatos de tacón alto　　**d.** Tampoco es una fiesta de disfraces.

4. ¿Qué ropa le parece a Karina "¡Perfecta!" para llevar?

_____

C **Todo junto**

1. *¡Nurvella y Noemí Blas van a celebrar sus quince años!* After watching this segment of the video several times, indicate which events you think were most important for making it a special day, with "1" marking your top choice. Compare your answers with several classmates. Were there one or two things that you all mentioned as your top choices?

   _____ Van a la iglesia en coche de caballo (una calandria).

   _____ Reciben regalos.

   _____ Llevan vestidos blancos bonitos hechos a mano.

   _____ Decoran la casa.

   _____ Bailan a la música de los mariachis.

   _____ Comen comida mexicana típica.

   _____ Comen un pastel grande.

2. *¿Qué están haciendo estas personas?*

   a. ¿Qué están haciendo las gemelas? _____

   b. ¿Qué están haciendo los invitados? _____

   c. ¿Qué están haciendo las personas cuando las gemelas están cortando el pastel?

   _____

3. *Ya vamos a decir "adiós" a Karina, Alexander, y Jorge y Gracia.* We have enjoyed several excursions with them in Guadalajara, Miami, and Madrid and you might by now have an impression of their personalities, likes and dislikes. Choose one of the hosts and write several paragraphs about your new acquaintance, describing (1) his or her appearance, (2) personality, likes and dislikes, and (3) a place or two that you have gone together. When you have finished, share your work with a classmate or file it in your portfolio.

   Here are some suggestions to help you get started:

   Ya conozco a un(a) muchacho(a) de. . . . Se llama . . .

   Acabo de decir "adiós" a mi nuevo(a) amigo(a) de . . .

   ¡Qué triste estoy! Debo decir "adiós" a mi amigo(a) . . .